D1378059

SINKHOLE

Also by Juliet Patterson
Threnody
The Truant Lover

SINKHOLE

A Legacy of Suicide

JULIET PATTERSON

MILKWEED EDITIONS

© 2022, Text by Juliet Patterson

All rights reserved. Except for brief quotations in critical articles or reviews, no part of this book may be reproduced in any manner without prior written permission from the publisher: Milkweed Editions, 1011 Washington Avenue South, Suite 300, Minneapolis, Minnesota 55415. (800) 520-6455 milkweed.org

Scripture taken from the New King James Version®. Copyright © 1982 by Thomas Nelson. Used by permission. All rights reserved.

Published 2022 by Milkweed Editions
Printed in Canada
Cover design by Mary Austin Speaker
22 23 24 25 26   5 4 3 2 1
First Edition

Library of Congress Cataloging-in-Publication Data
Names: Patterson, Juliet, author.

Title: Sinkhole : a legacy of suicide / Juliet Patterson.
Description: First edition. | Minneapolis, Minnesota : Milkweed Editions, [2022] | Summary: "A fractured reckoning with the legacy and inheritance of suicide in one American family"-- Provided by publisher.
Identifiers: LCCN 2022001973 (print) | LCCN 2022001974 (ebook) | ISBN 9781571311764 (hardcover) | ISBN 9781571317476 (ebook)
Subjects: LCSH: Suicide--United States.
Classification: LCC HV6548.U5 P38 2022 (print) | LCC HV6548. U5 (ebook) | DDC 362.280973--dc23/eng/20220421
LC record available at https://lccn.loc.gov/2022001973
LC ebook record available at https://lccn.loc.gov/2022001974

Milkweed Editions is committed to ecological stewardship. We strive to align our book production practices with this principle, and to reduce the impact of our operations in the environment. We are a member of the Green Press Initiative, a nonprofit coalition of publishers, manufacturers, and authors working to protect the world's endangered forests and conserve natural resources. *Sinkhole* was printed on acid-free 100% postconsumer-waste paper by Friesens Corporation.

Author's Note

This is partly a story of trying to understand suicide. This is also a story written through and about grief. In both cases, there are gaps to navigate—in memory, in access, and in the historical record—and so this book should be considered a work of creative nonfiction, although I have done my best to ground this work in geographical and historical research and the stories of others, as well as my own experience as I lived it. Specifically, the three imagined final days of my relatives—an attempt to understand the "transient tempest in the mind," as psychologist Edwin S. Shneidman calls suicide—while based in this research, do not represent actual transcriptions of thoughts or events.

Finally, I would like to note that this material may be difficult for some readers to encounter. If you or someone you know is in suicidal crisis, please call the National Suicide Prevention Lifeline at 1-800-273-TALK (1-800-273-8255).

JULIET PATTERSON'S FAMILY TREE

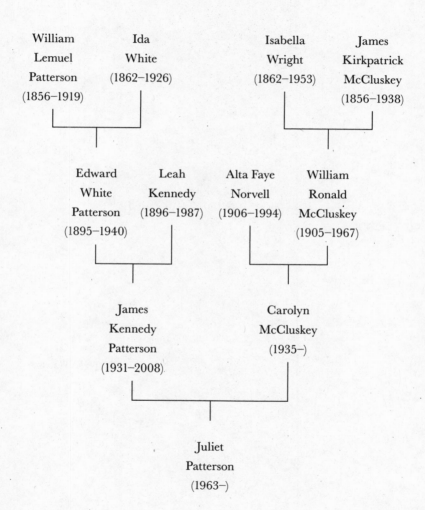

William Lemuel Patterson (1856–1919)

Ida White (1862–1926)

Isabella Wright (1862–1953)

James Kirkpatrick McCluskey (1856–1938)

Edward White Patterson (1895–1940)

Leah Kennedy (1896–1987)

Alta Faye Norvell (1906–1994)

William Ronald McCluskey (1905–1967)

James Kennedy Patterson (1931–2008)

Carolyn McCluskey (1935–)

Juliet Patterson (1963–)

I am working out the vocabulary of my silence.
— Muriel Rukeyser, "The Speed of Darkness"

And the end of all our exploring
Will be to arrive where we started
And know the place for the first time.
— T. S. Eliot, "Little Gidding," *Four Quartets*

PART

ONE

1.

Tuesday turns to Wednesday. December 17, 2008. The moon is almost in the last quarter. The sky is clear but pitch black. The temperature dips near zero, and already a foot of snow covers the ground in Minnesota. Coming home from work past midnight, my father swerves into the driveway somewhat carelessly, leaving his car pointed at an angle, a glove caught in the door. He enters the house through the garage door and descends into the basement, while my mother sleeps in the bedroom upstairs. He empties the contents of his pockets (keys, coins, cell phone) and removes everything from his money clip except his identification, which he leaves in his right rear pocket. He stands at the laundry utility sink and removes his dentures. He sits at his desk and writes a farewell note. He slips the note under the lid of the laptop computer on his desk and stacks several three-ring binders next to it.

He changes clothes. He pulls on a pair of long underwear and two sweaters, then an old winter coat, slightly torn at the sleeve. Before going out the door, he retrieves a small black sack that contains plastic bags, two box cutters, a pair of scissors, duct tape, cotton balls, and white nylon rope.

He walks outside, leaving the house through the garage, past the car in the driveway and into the street. He walks a block on Roy Street and turns left at Highland Parkway.

He walks a half mile down a long sloping hill, near two water towers and a sprawling golf course buried in snow. He turns right and walks another mile, along the east side of the golf course and into a park. Just before he reaches Montreal Avenue, he enters a small parking lot adjacent to a playground and a bridge that extends over the road. Here the snow is deep, and it slows him as he walks to the bridge's railing. From his sack, he takes one of the box cutters, the rope, and a plastic bag. Left inside is a note specifying his name and address. As he cuts the rope into two pieces, he accidentally nicks the thumb of his right hand. He makes two nooses. He ties the ropes to the railing and wraps the knots in duct tape. Then he climbs over the railing and stands on the concrete ledge, no more than a foot wide, overlooking a steep ravine. Below, to the left, a winding set of stairs is obscured by trees and snow. He pulls the plastic bag over his head and secures the nooses around his neck, tightening them just below his right ear. All of this takes only a matter of minutes.

My father chooses to die on the north end of the bridge. There, the canopy is so dense that, from the street, the structure appears to grow from the hill. In the dim light spreading from the railings, the crown of its arch bestows darkness.

When my father is found, nine inches of his right hand and wrist have frozen, though his trunk is still warm. The official time of death, 8:48 a.m., marks the moment when the police are dispatched to the scene, but the medical examiner estimates the actual time of death to be sometime between 2:00 and 3:00 a.m. My father hangs for nearly six hours through the night.

On the day my father died, a bitter cold wave swept across the northern regions of the country—snow and sleet fell from the Twin Cities, where we lived, to states on the Eastern Seaboard. It was midwinter, near the solstice, a time marked by the shortening of days.

I woke that morning feeling drowsy and hopeless, largely a side effect of the Vicodin I'd been given to relieve pain from injuries I'd sustained in a car accident. One week earlier, my car had been rear-ended by a taxi in a bottle-neck stretch of the I-94 freeway; the driver hadn't noticed that traffic ahead was slowing. I'd seen him careening toward me in the rearview mirror and knew I was going to be hit. Though I was lucky not to suffer any fractures or injuries to my spine, I had strained the upper vertebra known as the axis and damaged ligaments in my neck, chest, and upper and lower back. No bruises or cuts, just invisible and severe soft-tissue damage. It was difficult to sit; to stand; to concentrate, reason, or think. Without hydrocodone, I could feel the torn edges of muscle and tendon, the path of nerve needlelike in my arms.

As I cautiously rose, I realized that December 17 felt like a significant date, but I wasn't sure why. The only explanation was that, for the first time since the accident, I was planning to leave the house for something other than a medical appointment. I worked for a publishing sales group as an office manager, and my job involved not only clerical and administrative tasks but also physical labor—the office was a storehouse for the company's sales materials, including catalogs and books. After the accident, I had no choice but to take leave. Lifting boxes had become impossible, and sitting, at least for long periods of time, problematic. I was slated to return for a few hours that day. By the time the phone rang, however, I had already returned to bed with an ice pack, resigning myself to the fact that this wouldn't be happening. Listless, I could feel my body warming slightly from the morning's dose of medication, my heart slowing.

My mother's voice was strained. My father was missing from the house. I remember feeling an acute awareness of the burden that sometimes comes to an only child; she had no one else to call. I heard panic in her voice—a dire uncertainty—as though perhaps she already understood the meaning of his absence before the facts could be pieced together.

A few minutes later, she called again, hysterical; she'd discovered his suicide note underneath the lid of his laptop computer. *I have chosen to go on the north end of the footbridge over Montreal Avenue . . . near the steps I used to exercise on with the Beagles*, it said, delivered in an oddly casual syntax, as if he'd just gone out of the house on a quick errand.

My partner, Rachel, had already left for work. I called her office. She hadn't arrived yet, even though the walk was only a few blocks. Rather than waiting for her to receive my message, I rushed out of the house to find her. I took the rental car I'd been given following the accident, driving erratically under the influence of painkillers, and going only one block before I recognized the silhouette of Rachel's backpack and her familiar stride.

I have no memory of what I said to her as I climbed out of the driver's seat and she buckled herself in, nor do I have a memory of my 911 call, except that when I asked the dispatcher to summon police to the park, he told me they were already on the scene. I knew then that it was too late.

The police arrived at my mother's house moments after we did. No knock or bell—they simply walked in. One officer escorted my mother to the dining room table. The other stood with me just a few feet away in the kitchen, asking a battery of questions: *What's your relationship to the deceased? Any other relatives need to be notified? Are there other people you'd like us to call?* I stood with my father's suicide note in my hand, not reading, exactly, but rather occupying myself as I answered these questions, flipping the paper one way and then another, as if to make physical sense of it. Only in this moment, on the day he died, was I allowed to see and touch the note. The police would take it with them when they left, as evidence.

Morning news flared on a countertop television, mixing with the muted sounds of the officer's two-way radio. The moment unfurled in slow motion, the odd visual constraints of the kitchen shifting into a disjointed and chaotic landscape of sound—television, radio, the furnace fan bursting through a heater grate, the whisper-scrape of the police officer's jacket, and then his voice again. *You'll need to make arrangements with the coroner's office. Here's my card if you have any questions.*

The first officer went outside, and I left the kitchen and sat down on the dining room floor. The room spun. My mother sat at the table still dressed in a nightgown, leaning forward out of her chair. I heard the second officer, a woman, say, *I've seen a lot of these kinds of things—hundreds of scenes—some awful stuff.*

I felt bodiless and strange, as if I had lost contact with the ground. I watched yellow light unravel on the carpet and against the second officer's black shoe.

—He looked peaceful out there, she continued, *very clean. Peaceful.*

The house went quiet with an endless pause.

—Maybe that will help put your mind at ease.

I turned my face to the window. Across the yard, a neighbor's Christmas lights blinked in a row of junipers.

The day unraveled from there. A police chaplain came and went. A friend of my mother's arrived. Rachel made a trip to the store and brought back food to the house. I couldn't eat. By early afternoon, arrangements needed to be made. I telephoned the coroner, the funeral home. I answered questions I cannot recall. As the sun began to set and the day dimmed, I returned to the floor, lying on a pack of ice. Then, as we left my mother's house in the darkness, I asked Rachel to drive toward the park. We turned left on Montreal Avenue, down the hill that led to the bridge. The rise of the structure loomed on the horizon; the crown, haunch, and ribs flat in streetlight. At the sight of it, I wept.

In the weeks that followed, I returned to my feeling that the date was a significant one. December 17, I found, was both the Christian feast day of Daniel the prophet as well as Saturnalia, the ancient Roman festival honoring the deity Saturn. The biblical flood began on the seventeenth day, and in Greek superstition, it's considered the best day of the month to harvest timber for a boat. A haiku was often written using seventeen *onji*, or sound-symbols. Seventeen is an ominous number for Italians, considered the numerical equivalent of the Latin expression meaning "I lived," and, by extension, "I am dead."

————

Over the next few months, I realized that I didn't know my father very well; I had not spoken to him about things that mattered. There was a silence in him, and I had known, even as a very young child, that this was far more complex than a simple refusal of the past. It was, instead, a response to unthinkable grief, a coping strategy that forged a collective bond between my parents and placed large parts of the family history under taboo. We were all children of suicides. My father was eight when his father, Edward Patterson, took his own life, and my mother was thirty-two when her father, William McCluskey, did the same. If we rarely talked about important things, it was next to never that I heard them discuss their childhoods or my grandfathers. I knew little about those men or about the ways they had died.

Even before my father's death, I felt keenly the psychological burden of such an inheritance. My family seemed drawn to both suffering and shame, drawn to the idea that the world was one made of suffering and shame. My own vulnerability to depression had led me to therapy years ago, where I had begun to understand the elusive nature of trauma between generations and the messy collusion with history. After my father was gone and I felt his violent absence, I knew I needed to break open my family's silence. Who were these men? What led to these deaths in my family? What did my family's history of suicide imply? And what did it mean for my own future?

I can see now that, above all else, I was driven by a need to untangle myself from the strong ties suicide had attached to my life. I wanted to bring the past closer, to excavate a wound. Eventually, I came to the conclusion that if I did nothing else, at least I needed to uncover the stories long ago sealed in rock. Through the layers of sediment I began looking, grasping at dust.

2.

December 14, 2008, a Sunday, the last day I saw my father alive. He and my mother stopped by our house in the late afternoon, three days after my accident. As they arrived, I slowly made my way across the living room to the couch. I'd been confined to bed; I was weak, dizzy, and had difficulty walking. My vision blurred from medication. Yet I could still very clearly see my father as he came in through the entryway, and the huge flakes of snow in the window behind his head. He was wearing a baseball cap, a blue parka, and a pair of brown leather boots. No gloves, no scarf. A small man with a trim and muscular build, he looked much younger than his seventy-seven years, despite his white and thinning hair. An outsider might have mistaken him for a man who worked physical labor, partly because of the way he dressed and partly because of the way he walked with a subtle but recognizable swagger. But he was not that man. He was an office worker, a manager.

My father pulled his boots off by the heel and kicked them to the rug where other shoes were gathered. Rachel had opened the door to greet them and offered a closet hanger to my mother, who, after removing a pill-box hat constructed of synthetic fur, unzipped her coat. My mother gave Rachel a quick embrace, and from the couch I noticed that her thumb, chapped from the bitter cold, was cocooned in a bandage. It was on that bandage that my attention remained, until my mother caught sight of me on the couch and then seemingly burst into the room. I steadied myself and turned my body to face them, unable to rotate my neck under the constraint of a brace.

—*Why didn't you call us earlier?* she asked.

—*She's needed rest,* Rachel said, answering so I didn't have to.

My mother and father stood in the center of the room stiffly, visibly uncomfortable.

—*Why don't you sit down?* Rachel suggested.

Although Rachel and I had been together for four years, my parents still approached her with a certain degree of formality, even uneasiness. This was both their fault and my own. Since I had come out twenty years prior, my parents had meddled at all the wrong moments in my relationships. I was forty-five years old, but still trying to break free from the confines of being my parents' child. And so I had preferred, at least up until this point, to guard the privacy of my partnership with Rachel—a partnership that felt elemental, like bed-rock. As two writers, our relationship had been forged by creativity, and we stood guard, as the poet Rainer Maria Rilke once said, over the solitude of the other, a commitment not easily explained to my parents.

My mother ignored the invitation and remained standing in the middle of the room, rummaging through her handbag.

—*You need to get a lawyer,* she said.

My father sat down in a chair across the room as my mother removed a plastic bag from her purse. The bag was not only sealed but also wrapped in tape. Inside, she had packed a homeopathic analgesic for minor muscle and joint pain and a bottle of herbal pills meant to diffuse some side effects of Vicodin. Rachel offered tea and then left the room for the kitchen. A chain of questions from my mother subsumed the conversation: *How did it happen? Did you call your insurance agent? What did your doctor say? How will you get back to work?*

—*I've been in a lot of pain*, I replied.

—*And what about the car?* my mother continued. *How will you find another car?*

It was a few moments before I could speak.

—*I don't know. Maybe one will fall from the sky.*

Weary of her questions, I said this with sarcasm, which I now regret. My father remained quiet—but he was clearly listening. This phrase, these precise words, would come back in his suicide note: *Maybe Juliet will use the Volvo*, he would write in just a few days. *"A car from the sky"* she was waiting for.

When my parents left the house that evening, we walked them to the door. My father held on to my mother's arm as they moved out to the porch, down the sidewalk, and to the car. I watched them through the window, passing under the sweeping arm of a river birch in our front yard, two shadows in the blue light of winter.

After they left, Rachel and I drifted into another part of the house to watch a movie. When we returned to the living room before bed, it was frigidly cold. The front door hadn't been locked and the wind had blown it open.

Snow covered the threshold. A large ficus tree whose canopy had filled the corner of the entryway now sagged to the floor in ruin, branches bent and broken, blackened leaves strewn in every direction. I thought then of the tree as a strange harbinger of fortune, even a herald of death.

We didn't throw the tree away. We moved it from the entryway into another room, stripped it of every leaf, and cut it nearly down to the roots. The tree stood bare for months: apocalyptic, forbidding. Its bald, tangled branches sprang from the soil in what was now an enormous and oversized pot. Each time I passed by, I felt its humbled state mirrored my sense of grief and expectancy. More than once, I considered throwing the tree in the compost heap, but on every occasion, something stopped me; somehow my faith in it remained.

3.

Bridges surround me. About forty of them cross the Mississippi within the boundaries of Minneapolis and St. Paul. I live on the west bank of the river, within walking distance of four: a railroad bridge, a double-decked beam bridge (where the poet John Berryman jumped to his death in 1972), a concrete arch bridge bearing a freeway, and, finally, the I-35W box girder bridge that replaced the steel truss arch bridge that collapsed in 2007, toppling 108 feet into the river and riverbanks. If I leave my house for a walk (which I often do), I can find a bridge in nearly every direction.

Bridge #62075 (as registered in the Ramsey County record) was built in 1927 and adorned with Art Deco features; a sprawling arch suspended by massive footings and grates. It's a majestic but unassuming structure and doesn't cross water. For this reason, it is perhaps an unlikely suicide site: bridges are rarely used in suicide hangings. Trees are more common, though more often yet people hang themselves in their homes: attic, basement, garage, patio.

So what brought my father to the bridge? It is roughly one mile from my parents' house: in his younger years, my father routinely ran their dogs in the nearby park. He also used to exercise frequently by climbing the steps that

15

wound up and around the bridge's piers. He knew the bridge and its terrain well. It's easy to see how it might have occupied his imagination. And in choosing a public space, he might have been thinking of my mother, perhaps sparing her the trauma of discovering the body—or he might have thought he was less likely to be interrupted outside the house.

And why hanging? It's accessible. Quick. Simple yet highly effective.

———

The day after my father's death was bitterly cold. What began that morning as a disjointed business meeting upstairs at the Cremation Society of Minnesota—looking over a menu of services, completing paperwork for the death certificate, and, finally, choosing an urn—ended with the body. A dingy, flowered, oversized couch consumed one wall of the viewing room, located in the basement. Along the opposite stood two enormous fake palms and a torch lamp that leaned slightly in one direction. The harsh lighting underscored the futility of the room's greenery.

My father's body, when revealed, represented death in the purest sense. His face was crowned with small contusions. Blood vessels had broken on his temple, leaving a purple mantling down the side of his face. At first sight of him, I felt a momentary sense of relief, perhaps because the anticipation of this moment had come to an end. But as the minutes passed, I felt empty.

My mother paced in front of the body, holding Mickey, their shih tzu, under her arm. Animals—in particular, dogs, which they'd bred and showed—were a passion for my parents. Their dedication was often excessive; it sometimes seemed as if each of them valued animals over people. At the time of my father's death, Mickey had been their only pet for more than eight years and accompanied my mother virtually everywhere, to work and to social occasions. His presence at the viewing was, for us, nothing out of the ordinary.

She spoke to my father. First angrily, and then more desperately—*Why*, she asked, *why*, and then she held Mickey closer to my father's face. The dog sniffed the air and recoiled.

—*Let's go*, she said.

I was sitting on the couch.

—*I still need a minute*, I said.

My mother stepped outside the room, where the service director was waiting. They began speaking. I could hear their hushed voices through the wall. For a moment, I imagined the embalming room, neat and orderly, and my father lying there hours before, on a metal table: body scrubbed clean, eyes sealed, mouth sewn shut.

The body lay on a padded gurney, draped in a velvet cloth, with only my father's face visible. I knew he was naked underneath. Before entering the viewing room, the service director had explained that my father's clothes had been cut off by emergency responders and then, holding a tied plastic bag before us, asked if we wanted to keep what was left. My mother said no. I looked at the bag and could see only the vague outline of my father's shoes.

With my mother out of the room, I felt more relaxed, despite the difficulty of the moment. I stood up and moved close enough to touch the body. His hand first: cold. And then his head. He was gone. He did not exist. A feeling of immense sadness that I could not control welled up and caused me to emit a strange sound, something like a sob. I studied his face. His mouth twisted in a small grimace, and there were still traces of what I can only describe as determination across his brow. It struck me that I had seen hints of this expression in him many times before, though never so precisely. I closed my eyes for a moment. An image of a noose appeared, as though lying in wait. I opened my eyes. Without thinking, I lifted the cloth away from his neck. I had an impulse to know in more detail the circumstances of his death, to understand in clear terms the consequences on his body. The worst had already happened, so why not face it as best I could? With his neck finally exposed, I saw two deep furrows in his skin: one pale, the other yellow and hard. Later I read the coroner's report and learned the marks were consistent with *two separate ligature furrows*, with two individual nooses. It was a gruesome sight. I covered him as quickly as I could. I heard myself utter *I'm sorry* in an audible whisper, not so much an apology as a groan. I stepped out of the room.

My mother stood in a narrow hallway with the service director. He escorted us up the stairs and led us to the front door. As we stood in the entrance, my mother confirmed the schedule for cremation and the subsequent storage of my father's ashes for the winter—we wouldn't be burying him until spring, when she and I would drive to Pittsburg, Kansas, where they'd both been born. Per his will, there would be no funeral, though we'd plan for a small memorial service in Kansas. We shook the service director's hand and left.

Without speaking (had we earlier agreed to this?), my mother and I drove to the scene: the high footbridge at the edge of a wooded park in the heart of St. Paul. At the north end, where my father died, the bridge was flanked by a playground and a picnic area and stitched with trees. Underneath it, Montreal Avenue followed a valley that sloped toward the Mississippi. From where I stood on the bridge, I could only imagine the river. My mother, who had been standing behind me, wandered toward the playground with Mickey cradled under her arm. I turned and watched her set the dog down in the snow to pee. The temperature was so raw, his legs quivered and plumes of condensed vapor rose into the air above the pool of urine. When the dog finished, my mother picked him up again and walked toward the car in silence, tracing the shadows of other dull footprints. I followed, cutting another path through snow. Bulky clouds drifted above, and I watched as they passed out of sight, over a stand of maples. Suddenly, a dense storm of birds almost merged with the clouds and descended into the park, an aberrant chorus shearing the ambience of the day. I turned to look at my mother and pointed to the sky.

—*Look*, I said. But she couldn't see or hear me, the hood of her parka drawn over her head, her eyes low to avoid the glare of the sun.

It was a huge flock: one hundred birds or more. Trees teemed with birds. They flitted and dropped through the branches, calling out to each other in a fury. Everywhere I looked: birds. And not just any birds, but robins. Flocks of robins are itinerant, appearing only in periods of migration and usually only in the fall and winter—and seeing robins in December in Minnesota is unusual. Or, at least, had been unusual; I knew from reading about climate change that robins were appearing in a number of unexpected places. On Banks Island, about three hundred miles north of the Arctic Circle, they'd been spotted where they'd never been seen before.

———

When I was seven, my father brought home a nest of robin fledglings he'd found on the side of the freeway on his way from work. The nest had blown from a tree in a recent storm, and inside there were two or three birds struggling to stay alive. My mother made them a new, makeshift nest constructed of Easter grass, paper towels, and a plastic strawberry container. Because of her vigilance, one bird survived until morning.

Baby robins typically leave the nest when they are about two weeks old. After another ten to fifteen days, they are fully capable of flight and begin to live independently from their parents. As they grow, they need food every two to three hours during the daytime. For a solid month, my mother fed that bird by hand, chopping worms and fruit into a mixture that could be dispensed with an eyedropper. It was an exhausting task that she managed effortlessly.

When I was young, it wasn't unusual for my father to bring home injured or lost animals (he had a predilection for finding these creatures), nor was it out of the ordinary for my mother to care for them. She had a gift, a natural ability and inclination for rescuing wild animals. Our bird learned to fly in the house, often perching on curtain rods or doorframes, and eventually transitioned to experiments outdoors, lasting the better part of a day in our front yard. As the weeks went by, my mother was still feeding him, but less frequently, and now these sessions took place on the lawn instead of the kitchen counter. She called the bird by name—*Robbie*—in a singsong manner and taught him to associate this call with food. After a few days, as soon as my mother walked out the door making the call, the robin would fly to her. We brought the bird in at dusk for several weeks, but little by little, he began to take less food from my mother, and one night he stopped coming in the house altogether. Eventually, the robin stopped approaching us, though he often rested on a railing outside the back door. For two or three years, every spring, the bird returned. We knew he was our bird, because with my mother's call, we could summon him out of the trees to his familiar perch.

I remember the months we lived with the robin as a galvanizing period in my family's life. My mother, my father, and I were brought close together in the daily routine of attending to the bird. I felt that my family was uniquely important for having been given this task, proud—even at that young age—of the implications this had for my identity, and I found meaning in the fact that my family could truly enact earthly stewardship. All of this came to mind as I stood in the bitter cold of the parking lot the day after my father's death. It was still morning. The streets were empty, lifeless. My mother had settled herself in the car as I continued to watch the birds. In the weeks that followed, I thought back to this moment and looked for meaning in the flock—whether it was dates or birds, I was living by symbols, the only language I seemed to understand.

After we left the park, I took my mother home. As we pulled nearer to her house, I saw garbage bags stacked on the curb. A few days before my father's death, she had received a postcard from a local charity announcing a collection truck's visit to her neighborhood. She apparently had decided to take advantage of the opportunity this now presented, staying up through the night, without sleep, to pack up all of my father's belongings.

When I walked her inside, I learned that the only trace of my father still left in the house was a small box that held his last few objects: keys, a money clip, his driver's license, a wedding ring. I held the box in my hands briefly that morning, the contents meaningless and strange. My mother showed me a single black-and-white photograph cut from a photo strip, dated September 1, 1965. *He had this lying out a few weeks ago*, she said.

My mother is in the center of the photograph, a thin white bow in her hair. She holds me in her lap and looks into the camera with a vaguely dispirited expression on her face. I am almost two years old. My mother wears makeup: lipstick, mascara, and a small amount of eye shadow, precisely applied. She looks beautiful. I am not smiling. My father's face and body are barely visible. With his glasses removed, he looks withdrawn from the moment, like a person who's just unexpectedly moved into the frame. Only his right eye can be seen as he turns slightly toward the lens, his raised arm perfectly mimicking the slope of my mother's shoulder.

I asked my mother for the photograph. She passed it to me hastily. I slipped it into my wallet for safekeeping, and there it has remained, a private fetish. I have speculated many times as to why my father might have taken out this particular picture in the weeks leading up to his death. Maybe he simply unearthed it as he cleaned his desk, or maybe the choice was more significant: I'll never know.

What I do know is that my father methodically prepared for his death. He emptied his desk, gave away clothes, and discarded papers. He organized financial documents and left copious notes with instructions and advice related to the house, investments, and other matters, all bound in three-ring binders he left stacked on his desk. He prepaid his taxes and his cremation. He canceled his phone plan and carefully taped a note with the expiration date (one day after his death) to the back of his cell. These gestures are both comforting and deeply unsettling. Sometimes an oblique but generous feeling surrounds them, as if they demonstrate his willingness to help. In other moments, they feel secretive, cold, and detached. His various instructions, while informative, felt more like commands—*renew insurance on the car every May, pay estimated taxes quarterly using this payment schedule, the car is leaking oil*—as though my father were still trying to orchestrate the details of his life from the grave.

It's agonizing to think of how much thought he put into his end. Months after he died, I discovered a receipt for the cost of his cremation dated to October. As it turns out, this kind of advance planning isn't so unusual. According to psychologist Thomas Joiner, suicides (and suicide attempts) are likely to be highly thought out, with substantial planning and preparation, even if these activities are unknown to everyone around the person in question. While it might be easier to think of suicide as an impulsive act, the real truth is impulsive suicides are rare: usually there's a plan.

But who dies by suicide? And how does suicide happen? For decades, theorists have tried to understand it. Some have focused on psychological pain, others on social isolation, and yet others on a sense of escape or hopelessness. While these theories have guided suicide research and prevention in significant ways, they have also limited our understanding of suicide, as few, if any, have succeeded in "differentiat[ing] explanations for suicidal thoughts and suicidal behavior." As people who think about killing themselves don't always follow through, it raises a crucial question: How does ideation turn to action?

Significant progress in suicide theory was made in 2005, when Joiner outlined a new framework to address this query. Joiner's theory suggests that people who commit suicide share three common traits. The first is loneliness, the second is feeling like a burden, and the third is the acquired capacity for self-harm.

Joiner represents a new generation of suicide experts. His own father died by suicide, and his theoretical approach, while based in clinical research, is also deeply personal. "A nagging fact about my dad left me unsatisfied with existing theories of suicide," Joiner writes, "and pushed me to think in new ways about his death and about suicide in general." Elsewhere, he has said that he is "honor-bound" to not only understand suicide but to "exact some revenge for it—something or somebody stole my dad away from me, is the way I view it."

I imagine my father seated in the living room of my house on that last visit just three days before his death. Were all of his plans made? The day chosen? He waits with a glass of water resting on his thigh in his right hand. His pants are pulled high from sitting, revealing gray wool socks with a gold toe seam. He's wearing a rust-orange shirt, one I gave him on a previous Christmas, and khaki trousers. I am lying on the couch, my head turned against an ice pack. What I can see most clearly are his feet, hips' distance apart, planted squarely on the ground. I am in enormous pain, beyond his help. What can this possibly mean for a father? I am not sure I know. When I find myself speculating, I have to dismiss the matter to preserve myself from sadness.

When I returned to the car, I sat thinking about the garbage bags filled with the last of my father's possessions: belongings he himself had decidedly left behind. Whatever had escaped his preparations was probably not significant. Still, I regret the decision I made next: I left the bags in the snow. I had neither the nerve nor the presence of mind to do otherwise. My mother had made it clear that she was on the side of distance and forgetting. She would have been startled by the very idea that I might claim my father's possessions against her will. And so, between the abandoned clothes at the Cremation Society of Minnesota and the bags on the curb, that morning took with it the chance to touch the last traces of my father's earthly presence.

Psychiatrists Terry Martin and Kenneth Doka have emphasized a scale of grief with two distinct patterns on each end. The intuitive pattern is an emotional expression of grief, while the instrumental is expressed physically or cognitively. With the capacity to feel a large range of emotions, intuitive grievers are less able to think through the pain of grief, and more likely to appear overwhelmed and wrecked by it. Instrumental grievers most often seek information and facts and prefer to take action; they may speak of grief in a rational way and appear to others as cold or absent of feeling.

In the wake of my father's death, my mother had been waylaid by emotion. That day, she could not bring herself to think about the terrible thing that had happened. Nor to speak of it, nor to have it in her head or home.

4.

My father didn't like being photographed. I don't have many pictures of him, and the ones I do have are more than thirty years old. In these portraits, he's a young man I can't remember very well. How can that be? He was the one who taught me to tie my shoes, ride a bike, swing a tennis racket, read a map. He taught me how to play chess, how to wash a car, how to turn a key inside a lock. He was the one who held up flashcards at the dinner table, the one who most often helped me with homework, the one who fixed broken toys. He was the one who volunteered for school field trips, who chaperoned a cold winter slumber party in an igloo we'd built in science class. Meanwhile, my mother took care of the necessities. She did all the cooking, and when I was old enough to go to school, she packed my lunch every day. She knew when it was time to buy new shoes, alter the hem on a pair of jeans, cut my hair. She was the one who scrubbed grass stains from my clothing or purchased me new socks and underwear.

But despite her care, my father was the tireless parent, the one most willing, even after a long day of work, to indulge the whims of my imagination. A particular role I cast him in when I was very young was that of a hungry giant, especially fond of eating little girls. Cursed with poor eyesight, the giant had to rely primarily on his sense of smell to find his dinner. He stumbled around the house making terrifying groans as I hid under furniture, out of his reach. At other times (especially while driving in the car), his hands became live crabs sent to crawl over my legs and arms. Before I went to bed, he made shadow puppets on the wall: rabbits, deer, and butterflies.

As an only child, I defended these moments with my father carefully. They were fleeting, not only because eventually a parent must be a parent (and cease to be one's companion) but also because of my father's emotional unpredictability, which only seemed to increase over time. At turns sullen and secretive, or remote and cutting—hot-tempered when angry and melancholy when hurt—he could inspire both fear and confusion in me. In my adolescence, these feelings grew, and the emotional distance between us deepened. My tomboyishness, which he had relished when I was a child, had become an aberration. Talking with him became more difficult: even the simplest conversation could be a source of stress, where I grew increasingly upset and he either met me with silence or cut me off with unsolicited advice. As a consequence, he did his most crucial communicating through letters, pushed under the lip of a door, propped on a bed pillow, or, in more urgent occasions, slid across the dinner table. In the course of my life, he wrote to me more than half a dozen times this way: sometimes as an expression of love, sometimes as an admonition, and sometimes, again, as an opportunity to dispense unwanted advice. Articulate and well written, these letters showed me a side of my father I otherwise wouldn't have known.

I regret that I didn't save these letters. I burned most of them in my early twenties after my father had written to me in response to my coming out, in a letter he slipped near my dinner plate the night before I was headed to Europe for a six-week backpacking trip. I was home for the summer, about to start my senior year of college, and the trip was the result of a year of scrimping and saving. I didn't read the letter until I was on the plane. I remember it was short, no more than two pages, a declaration of disappointment and disgust at my *deviant lifestyle* and a startling admission that when in the army as a young man, he, too, had been encouraged *by a bunk mate toward that dark tunnel* but had had the courage to say no. *There's no getting out of the tunnel*, he wrote. Enclosed in the envelope was a check for two thousand dollars, the full amount of a savings account he'd started for me as a child, with a note that said, *The last bit of support you can expect from me. You're on your own now.*

When I returned from the trip, I cashed the check. I left my parents' house and moved out of state and into my own apartment. I didn't speak to my father for more than a year. I burned the letter and all the others I had saved. It seemed easier to destroy than to preserve any memory; wasn't this what I'd learned from my father, after all?

———

I have kept only one letter from him. He wrote it decades ago, when I was near the end of a long-term relationship, a breakup I initiated. By this time, he had long since made peace with my sexuality. Though my father knew little about my choice to leave the relationship—we didn't talk then or later about such intimacies—he felt very strongly that I was making a mistake. He tried to persuade me to change my mind, opening with one of the interpretations of chapter sixty-four of the *Tao Te Ching*: *People usually fail when they are on the verge of success. So give as much care to the end of the beginnings, then there will be no failure.*

My father continues:

I love you very much. I think you are a wonderful person and very intelligent and compassionate.

I have told you several times that I think that the love I see that you have for A. and that she has for you is extraordinary. Mom has a little plaque somewhere that says love is like a UNICORN—rare and beautiful.

I think it is good for both of you to be committed to each other and to change and grow together within that context.

You are very driven in your Art—and in your thinking about the world and your existence.

My limited insight into things like the mind and such, gives me pause to speak. My intuition tells me to.

I haven't always been really relaxed about life— chopping wood and carrying water perhaps has taken too much of my energy.

The letter goes on to say, *The Tibetans speak of four faults, which prevent us from realizing the nature of our mind right now.* Next, my father outlines and numbers these faults, quoting from a source he chooses not to name, but which I imagine to be something like *Introduction to Tibetan Buddhism.* He writes, *The nature of the mind is just too close to be recognized. It is too profound for us to fathom; it is too easy to believe; it is too wonderful to accommodate.*

When I read this letter now, it's hard to imagine him writing it—hard to imagine him browsing through the pages of the *Tao Te Ching* or Buddhist texts, hard to imagine him choosing passages, hard to imagine him underlining, numbering, or emphasizing particular phrases with the nose of his pen. Where would these books have come from? My father knew I appreciated Buddhist teachings. I had read many books on the subject and for a number of years maintained a steady meditation practice. Was he trying to speak a language he thought I might understand? Or did he have his own buried spiritual convictions?

He goes on:

> I think realizing the scope of love is similar to
> seeking enlightenment. In Tibet, I guess people routinely
> commit themselves to realizing this enlightenment.

> I think that if you commit to your relationship with each
> other—relax in that commitment is the right thing for
> your life.

> I love you always,

> Dad

It is painful to read this now. His sentiment is beautiful and even profound, but to this day I'm annoyed by his meddling. It had taken him years to accept the fact that I was gay, and when he finally did, he seemed to disapprove of nearly all of my romantic partners. A. was different: he loved her, even adored her. Even now, I'm not entirely sure why. Not because A. wasn't beautiful, intelligent, and charismatic—she was—but because he had been so hard to please. It makes sense that the moment I made a decision for myself, he'd try to intervene. On the other hand, it's hard not to be moved. There is a tenderness and sadness in his disclosure: *I am writing to tell you how I'm feeling*; *I haven't always been relaxed about life*; *I think realizing the scope of love is similar to seeking enlightenment.*

This letter, to me, is expressive of my father's paradoxes. His inner life, based on our conversations, seemed almost nonexistent—but his letters suggested otherwise. He couldn't talk about it, so he wrote about it. Or else gave it away to the silence that seemed to fill our house.

5.

Christmas. My father had been dead for one week. His body had been cremated and the death certificate for him—James Kennedy Patterson—signed. I don't remember crying, though a medical visit a few days before the holiday revealed additional strain and swelling in my neck that had been caused, the doctor reasoned, by the effort of tears. Despite the decline in my physical condition, she encouraged me to proceed with a trip we had planned to visit Rachel's family in Massachusetts, if for no other reason than to begin to return life to normalcy.

My mother, Rachel, and I spent Christmas at the house of friends who lived in St. Anthony Park, a neighborhood bounded by the University of Minnesota's St. Paul campus and the Minnesota State Fairgrounds. They made a lavish holiday feast, though I didn't eat: there were plates of meat, greens, vegetables, and sweets; trays of cookies and wine; and a table set with fine china, silver, and delicate crystal. The table stretched at full extension through the open arch of the dining room and into the living room, where a large fir tree trimmed with ornaments stood. At our own house, we didn't have a tree. Wrapped presents were stacked on a table near a centerpiece of pine boughs. Everything I had meant to give to my father, I later gave away.

We left the Christmas party early and drove without talking away from the house, down Como Avenue. We were in my father's car, the one that had fallen from the sky, a vintage Volvo station wagon. My mother had insisted I take it. I had done so reluctantly. Though I felt attached to the Volvo as one of my father's few remaining possessions, the sight of it also filled me with dread. I'd been a passenger in the car dozens of times before, my father at the wheel. When I drove it, I could feel tangible traces of him that had otherwise vanished; the interior bore his scent, the steering wheel an ointment from his hands. I could see the streaks where he had wiped the dashboard clean with water. I could feel the worn surface of the floor mat where his heel had repeatedly settled, the slight hollow of his body in the driver's seat.

It wasn't just my father's presence that made me reluctant to take the car. After the accident, I'd become afraid of driving. So in the days following my father's death, I abstained from Vicodin and got back behind the wheel to face my fear. It wasn't a good decision. Without medication, I was left ragged with pain.

That night, as I drove, I felt a stabbing ache at the base of my skull and a gnawing stiffness in my body. It was already pitch dark. The night was overcast and there was little traffic. We'd driven only a few blocks when I saw something in the middle of the road. As we drew nearer, a man rushed into the street, waving his hands, gesturing for us to stop. I pulled to the shoulder. In the blinking glow of my hazard lights, I realized the thing in the road was a woman.

Rachel, my mother, and I got out of the car. We wavered in the street for a few seconds before another man approached and knelt on the ground by the woman. I moved forward, following suit. Other cars pulled off the road. A small group of people gathered. The young woman was lying on her back, her black hair spread on the asphalt. She was wearing pajamas and a nylon jacket, slippers on her feet. Because they were startlingly out of place in the bitter temperature, the slippers are what I remember in detail. Plush white, open-heeled, crowned with a collar of shearling, they made her bare ankles appear smaller and more delicate than they actually were. And they made of her feet an oversized cartoonish parody. The image was a mixture of tragic and comic: toes pointing to the sky, heels laced with snow and ice.

The man spoke to the woman as he removed his coat and draped it over her.

—*Have you been hit? Are you all right?*

There was no answer.

The woman's skin was sallow, her breathing labored, her gaze limp and unfocused. I took her hand. For an instant, I believed I could help her. The man yelled into the crowd, asking someone to call for an ambulance, even as he stared intently at the woman. Still reeling and raw from the events of the past week, I instantly understood the scene not as accident, but rather as aborted suicide.

Before long, paramedics arrived. As they approached, I dropped the woman's hand and stood to my feet. I felt both anxious and relieved. The paramedics rushed her to the ambulance, breaking the chain of people gathered in the street to protect her. Many of us watched as they seated her at the back of the ambulance and began a sequence of rudimentary diagnostics. They shone a light in her eyes, took her blood pressure, listened to her heartbeat. And as they finished, the woman jumped out of the ambulance and ran into the snow. Blankets flew into the street. The paramedics caught her and carried her back. This time, they put her on a gurney and strapped her down. I couldn't hear what they were saying, so I watched their faces. I remember one glancing at the other before he began asking questions. From the woman, still no response.

A police car arrived. An officer stood in the middle of the road with a bullhorn in his hand.

—*All right, thank you—everyone can go home now*, he said, waving a hand in the air.

When the crowd began to disperse, the ambulance with the woman inside disappeared down the street. We were a few blocks from the fairgrounds. In the distance, I could see the frames of empty cattle barns, the silhouette of a towering space needle in the sky. Rachel and my mother surfaced from the crowd and walked with me back to the car without saying a word.

I went to sleep that night only after taking a sedative. Until then, anxious thoughts kept me up, and the night was long. Instructions given with the medicine warned of drowsiness: *You may still feel sleepy the morning after taking this medicine. Wait at least four hours or until you are fully awake before you do anything that requires you to be awake and alert.*

We left for the airport early the next morning. At that point, I was primarily managing pain in my neck and lower back with ice packs, but as soon as my sedative wore off that day, I took Vicodin. In addition to my still-healing injuries, I also carried physical symptoms of grief. I wasn't eating much or sleeping well; my mind raced; I often felt dizzy. It was more than a five-hour trip from Minneapolis to Cape Cod, including a two-hour bus ride from Boston to Falmouth; the Vicodin helped me sleep, thwarting nerve signals and obscuring the spasmodic movements of the bus, but when we finally arrived, the pain was so acute, I vomited in the bathroom of the bus station.

We stayed at a house near the beach, a few miles away from where Rachel's mother lived. The house belonged to a family friend, away for the winter. I was grateful to have the privacy. There, I began writing these pages. I worked slowly, but with an odd sense of urgency. With Minnesota and my father's death at a physical remove, I tentatively started to feel that I was turning a corner.

That tenuous peace fractured a few days after Christmas, when Rachel discovered she was pregnant. That afternoon, she had driven me to a friend's house in Provincetown, where I spent a few hours on a couch, trying to string together a narrative of recent events. I convulsed in sobs and tears. Rachel, meanwhile, went to visit another friend across town. She stopped at a drug-store first and took a pregnancy test in the company of her friend. It was perhaps for the best that I was not the first to share in Rachel's news. I had been deeply ambivalent about becoming a parent and, in the wake of recent events, was not prepared to take in anything joyous or life-affirming the way that a pregnancy so excitedly, delicately, is. Instead, later, she and I stood together on the invisible threshold of parenthood in the cramped bathroom of her mother's house, where she showed me the positive test.

I imagine looking down on the scene from above: Rachel fingering the pregnancy wand as I stared at a hand towel hanging near the sink. It was pressed and folded neatly—like something you might find in a hotel—and embroidered with shells. Robust and pastel, they looked nothing like the bay scallops you might find in the local eelgrass beds, and I found this discrepancy irritating. Looking back, however, I can see the true source of my irritation was the sheer timing of events. *Why now?*

The pregnancy should not have been a surprise. We'd begun the process of insemination just months before my father's death but kept it quiet, wanting to be sure a pregnancy had taken before we shared the news. My parents never knew our plans. Impossibly, we had scheduled an insemination the day of the car accident. Postponing the procedure was not an option—timing was everything. When our doctor arrived at the house that evening with sterilized instruments wrapped in a dish towel inside her purse, I was lying flat on my back with an ice pack. I had to stand up and hold a flashlight to assist, and my hand trembled with pain. From the beginning, things seemed fraught with difficulty.

The news of Rachel's pregnancy was mixed for another reason; we had spent more than a year locked in conflict over the possibility of having a child. Rachel knew with certainty that she wanted to be a mother, but

I had never imagined myself as a parent. I didn't want the responsibility; I wasn't interested in children, and I was terrified of losing solitude and creative time, of relinquishing the thing that brought me the most joy.

I opened the bathroom door and slipped out into the hall. Rachel followed me into the living room. I got down on the floor with an ice pack and closed my eyes as she went into the kitchen to share the news with her mother. I stared at the ceiling. I might have fallen asleep. I might have only imagined sleep. At one point, the sun burst through a bay window and cast a glaring light on my face.

Later that day, Rachel and her mother, giddy with excitement, announced a celebratory shopping trip. I politely refused an invitation to come along. They returned a few hours later with a bag of baby accessories—a blanket, boots, and a pair of onesies. Her mother opened a bottle of champagne, and an infant's shape emerged on the carpet as Rachel laid out their purchases. Seven weeks later, she would lose the baby in a miscarriage, fall into her own broken state. But for the moment, there was a dream of a future for Rachel, full of possibility. So whatever grief I felt then, whatever trepidation, I tried to keep to myself. Though I'm not certain Rachel or her family understood, I began to excuse myself from gatherings and instead spent time alone in the rented house as a matter of necessity. Rachel and I had never been farther apart—spiritually, emotionally, physically—than we were in those weeks— and if solitude was a need, the distance also held a private agony for each of us.

It was a cold winter in New England, and in that week we spent on the Cape, there were two big storms. One morning, in the midst of one of these storms, I sat at a small table in the living room and watched snow fall as though it would never stop. Rachel had left hours before to spend the day with family. I'd already gone through my routine of ice packs, but it wasn't enough. I turned back to painkillers, hoping to block everything out. I pulled all the shades and wandered around the house. In the basement, I found an artist's studio filled with paper, chalk, and paints. I rummaged through bins of old magazines. I tried to read. I sat at the table. I carried a large sketchbook up to the living room. I scribbled the paper black with a ballpoint pen. Hours passed. I lay on the couch. The bed, the floor. Then, finally, in the center of an attached greenhouse. The greenhouse had a small door, and as I entered, I felt the heat of the room mop my skin. Cluttered with lemon and palm trees and a vast assortment of exotic orchids and lilies, the room held the clean and sharp aroma of blossom and dirt. As I stood there, surrounded by the pungent smell of soil, watching snow fall through the greenhouse's glass ceiling, a physical sensation of numbness swept over me suddenly, blocking out sight and sound. Things went dark. The world seemed to be slipping away. I would not have described myself as suicidal, but in that moment, suicide felt like a threat. I'd long reasoned that, given the legacy of suicide in my family, I'd somehow be protected from losing either of my parents that way. Now the door had opened and I felt a new fear: suicide as a prospect for me.

This was what was on my mind at the close of that week on the Cape. Not long after, I checked the online guestbook for my father's obituary. Fifteen people had signed it, including one anonymous sender:

—*I pray you've found peace in the loving arms of God*, he wrote.

—*How did you know my father?* I responded in the comments.

—*I found him; I've been praying for him. And now I will pray for you*, he replied.

Upon further inquiry, I learned he was a student at Highland Park High School, the same school I'd once attended, just a few blocks away from the park where my father died. He'd discovered the body on his way to school. I'm not sure how he knew my father's name or found the obituary—perhaps he called the police and asked. Or perhaps he checked the small black sack my father left on the bridge.

Sometimes, even now, I imagine him: the boy in the park, crossing the street to reach the steps near the bridge, head bent to shield his eyes from the biting cold and what awaited him just above.

6.

Seven days after my father's death, I began to pray. I made
a small altar for him in my study—photographs, candles,
a bowl of water—and prayed there every Wednesday,
all the way through December, January, and part of
February. Forty-nine days of winter.

As a child, I was never asked to pray. We weren't a
religious family. I was asked instead to think of something
that had made me happy during the day, which over the
years had become a habit and then a ritual, less prayer
than meditation. As an adult I transformed this into my
own lay Buddhist practice of chanting mantras, often re-
hearsed silently in bed. I knew, from this practice, that in
Tibetan Buddhism both mantras and prayers are considered helpful to the dead, as death is believed to occur in
stages, a process of reincarnation. And so, for my father
I repeated a familiar Buddhist mantra—*Om mani padme
hum*, six syllables that became my blessing for him, for the
body of the dead.

Every Wednesday after my prayer ritual, I spent long
hours on the couch, looking out on the street and resting
my pained neck. I often imagined the Mississippi, a few
blocks away, topped by the pale rectangles of high-rise
apartments; lined by the white streetlamps of the road;
closed off, in either direction, by a bridge.

One day, it occurred to me that I hadn't yet looked through the binders of notes and instructions my father had left behind, which suddenly seemed like an obvious oversight. I drove to my mother's house with irrational urgency, repeating the drive Rachel and I made on the day my father died. When I arrived, she greeted me at the door. Even though my father had been dead for weeks, we were both still in shock.

—*Are you coming in?*

—*Sure*, I said, *but I can't stay long.*

I entered the back hallway landing. From where I stood, I could see down a set of stairs into the basement, see the small dome of a reading light and a stack of papers on the surface of what used to be my father's desk.

Six months before his death, my father had fainted, hit his head, and fallen partway down those stairs. It was near midnight, and he'd just arrived home from the swing shift. He insisted, after he came to, that he'd slipped on the landing. But after a trip to the emergency room and admittance to the hospital, his doctors determined the fainting was a likely symptom of heart disease, something he'd been diagnosed with seven years earlier.

He was stubborn. Back then, he lived with severe chest pain for several months before revealing his problem to my mother. She insisted he consult a physician, and he was given a battery of tests and the prognosis that his heart could collapse in two years if left untreated. The treatment for his condition required a full valve replacement, a surgical procedure that had a long history of good results for patients. But it was a course of action my father feared. He was skeptical of invasive procedures and distrustful of Western medical doctors, especially surgeons, whom he seemed to think were only interested in making money. Despite the numerous conversations my mother and I had with him on the subject, he refused the recommended treatment. Instead, he became convinced that his best course of action was a crash program in megavitamin therapy and exercise, an organic approach to a mechanical problem, destined to fail.

After he fainted, my father sat on the edge of his bed dressed in a hospital gown, his feet suspended in the air, shaking his head. A cardiologist arrived and noted the elevated levels of niacin in his blood.

—*You've certainly beaten the odds*, he said. *I can see from your medical records that you were diagnosed with stenosis some years ago—but you're taking enough niacin to kill an elephant.*

Niacin is a B vitamin that causes the blood vessels to dilate near the skin, reduces blood fats and clears arteries. Niacin is commonly prescribed in small doses to patients with high cholesterol, but it's necessary to take the medication with the supervision of a doctor, given the long list of potential side effects: abnormal heart rhythms, diarrhea, dizziness, fainting, flushing, headache, heartburn, nausea, and vision loss due to toxic reactions, to name a few. My father had been taking his niacin supplement in secrecy, the most recent addition to his self-designed health regime.

The doctor paged through records on a clipboard.

—It may have helped you up until now, but the fainting bothers me. We often consider fainting to be a progressive symptom of heart disease, but in this case, the number of pills you were taking could have just as easily caused it.

As I stood in the hallway of my parents' house, remembering this, my mind veered to one detail from the coroner's report, listed under "Medications": *four probable vitamin pills accompany the body.*

My mother's voice interrupted my thoughts.

—Is this what you wanted? she asked, pulling wide the handles of a paper bag to reveal three large binders.

—Yes.

—I can't lose any of these things, she said. *You'll need to keep them in your house. I hope you don't find any loose ends in here.*

When my father died, my mother had little to no knowledge of their financial situation. He had always taken care of those things. As she was overwhelmed by the staggering sum of forms, finances, and paperwork involved in closing his affairs, I would soon become my father's executor, taking much of the burden away from her. Still, for many months after his death, she lived in fear that something was incomplete, unfinished, or, worse, incorrect.

—There's nothing to worry about, I said.

And that was true. My father's substantial life insurance policy was settled quickly, leaving my mother with enough money to live very comfortably. The policy had been something of an issue for him: a few months before he died, he told me that his ten-year term was set to expire at the end of the year, tripling his premium to roughly seven thousand dollars annually. He didn't want to pay and complained bitterly about the cost. But while it wasn't a small sum of money, I didn't understand why he so adamantly opposed paying it.

I left my mother's house that afternoon with the binders and brought them back to my study. As I perused them, I learned his overall financial situation was grim. Although he was working at the time of his death, he had actually retired early, in 1986, from a job at Northwest Airlines, taking advantage of a substantial compensation offered in a merger. Just three years later, at the age of sixty-eight, he returned to a full-time position at a data recovery company. He claimed he missed working. I believed him. It never crossed my mind that he might have needed the money. My father was remarkably frugal, with spending behavior bordering on stingy. While never a very wealthy man, he had always aspired to save his way to riches. And yet, now, there were surprisingly few assets.

I examined the documents as a private investigator might, scouring my father's handwritten notations for an explanation of the obvious loss of money. There was nothing but a few long and discursive descriptions of some high-risk investments.

At that moment in time, the world's financial system was in turmoil. The stock market crash of September 2008 marked the beginning of the largest decline since the Great Depression. If you didn't hold on to your stock, it was easy to relinquish money. Lehman Brothers went bankrupt. Merrill Lynch, AIG, Freddie Mac, Fannie Mae, and others all came within a hair of doing so and had to be rescued. Western leaders injected billions of dollars into the banking system to prevent a complete world collapse, but the effects of the crisis were nevertheless cataclysmic. The United States lost 8.7 million jobs and economic growth fell to a standstill, and there were more painful costs yet: the crash of 2008 led to a spike in suicides among men. One study calculates more than ten thousand suicides tied to the crisis in Europe and North America. Had my father, I wondered, been one of the lost?

When I tried to gain access to the account history of his stock holdings, I was denied. My mother, as sole beneficiary, was the only one who could legally request those statements. I didn't have the nerve to ask her. I had the sense she wouldn't want to know the truth of their affairs. It was the same with bank accounts. I searched his laptop for the lost history of documents, files, and photographs—anything that might contain some kind of information related to finances. I found nothing. I hacked into his email account by guessing his password (the name of his favorite beagle). Still nothing. My father had wiped his computer clean. All he'd chosen to leave behind were the binders sheathed in royal-blue vinyl, organized by subject: house, car, finances, insurance, and taxes. In the weeks that followed, I scoured those binders again and again, in search of an answer to the question: Why did he do it? I was looking for a narrative, one that supplied a simple motivation.

With the money trail run dry, I turned to my father's life insurance policy. He'd annotated the document with notes, including instructions on what to do if the policy somehow failed. I read the policy repeatedly, as if it might reveal something new. Its single exclusion was a suicide clause, valid only for the first two years of contract, during what's referred to as the "contestability period." The clause provides protection for the insurance company against people taking out a large amount of life insurance and then committing suicide in order to improve their family's financial position. My father appeared to have done his research: he not only highlighted the clause in his copy of the policy, but also attached a xeroxed copy of a Minnesota statute protecting against denial of payment, just in case there was some kind of trouble. But, in the end, the insurance company hadn't contested my mother's benefits. The money had paid out, and paid out quickly.

The scant assets, the annotated policy—what my father left behind clearly suggested part of the story. But what he didn't leave behind, the parts of his life that he had carefully excised, meant I would never know the whole of it. Eventually, I put the binders aside. They said something, but a silence remained.

PART

TWO

7.

At some point in the week following my father's suicide, my mother gave me a small folder she'd found in his nearly empty desk. I don't remember the reason. I may have asked her about stray documents, or perhaps she'd simply cleaned out his desk: one more purge. The folder contained two newspaper articles related to my paternal grandfather's death. Years before, my father had copied them at the Pittsburg Public Library in Crawford County, Kansas, during a trip for his mother's funeral.

I hadn't gone with my parents to Pittsburg, and when they returned home, my mother told me only in passing that my father was doing some family research. When I pressed further, she said he'd been looking into his father's death. I knew not to ask any more questions. But a few days later, my father appeared at my office in St. Paul, holding a folder fat with newspaper clippings. When I saw him in the doorway that afternoon, I was overcome with dread. He'd never visited me at work before; he hadn't called in advance, and the timing of the visit was awful. I was alone in the office that day and a full pallet of sales catalogs had just been delivered. Boxes clogged the entryway, the phone rang endlessly, and I was in the middle of repairing a fax machine. My father seated himself in a chair and, without a hello, began shuffling through the papers he set in his lap.

—*I've got something to show you*, he said, holding up one of the newspaper articles. *I've discovered something really interesting.*

—*What's that?* I asked.

I moved closer to see a handful of xeroxes. At the top of the pile was a half-page newspaper photograph. The shot captured my father in midair, a basketball rolling off his fingertips. Later, I found a dozen articles in the *Pittsburg Morning Sun* covering the pictured game. The year was 1948. My father was seventeen years old. And in the closing minutes of the game, he'd scored the basket that brought his team to victory. It was the first time the Pittsburg High School varsity basketball team won the Southeast Kansas League regionals.

—*Is that you?* I asked.

—*That's not what I wanted to show you. That's not important. This*, he said, holding up a page of handwritten notes attached to a copy of another article, *is what's important. My father was murdered. I can prove it.*

The phone on my desk started to ring and I ignored it, waiting for what he might say next.

—*It's all right here*, he added, slipping the paper back into the folder and closing it shut.

Minutes seemed to pass as I struggled to think of a response. I regret, now, that I didn't drop everything and give him my full attention. But in the moment, a mixture of anger and anxiety kept me from responding. Why here? Why now?

During my own childhood, my father never told any stories about his father, Edward, nor about his death. No one, in fact, ever talked about my grandfather. And if asked a question about Edward, my father would consistently say, *I don't want to talk about it.*

—*I'd love to hear more*, I said, *but I'm wondering if we can do this another time?*

My father said nothing.

The phone rang again, this time more difficult to ignore. I thought for a moment of announcing this fact, then realized it wasn't important. But what was important?

—*I'm really distracted—I've got a meeting across town—*

—*Right*, he said, standing up and turning toward the door.

—*Dad, wait*, I said. *Another time? We could have lunch or something.*

—*Sure*, he said, but he was already almost out the door.

A day or so later, I made sure to set a date with him. I knew that if I allowed too much time to lapse, our window would close. My father and I agreed to meet for lunch the following week. But I was late for that appointment, unable to call my father, who didn't yet own a cell phone. He didn't wait: when I arrived at the restaurant, he was already gone.

—*You were late. I didn't have time to wait*, he said when I called him at home.

—*I'm so sorry. Can we make another date?*

—*We'll see*, he said.

I tried a few more times to arrange lunch. My father always had an excuse, and eventually I gave up. I interpreted his refusal as punishment, but it is equally valid to think that he might have impulsively crossed his own line regarding privacy when he showed up at my office. Once the moment was lost, it was lost forever, even to him.

Until my father died, I had never really seen a picture of my grandfather Edward. So much shame surrounded the circumstances of his death. I'd only learned the story of his suicide through my mother, and she herself knew only snippets of the full narrative, which she told me in my late teens. One day, when she and my father were first together, he'd taken her on a country drive. He slowed the car near a certain spot, stopped, said something as simple as *My father killed himself there*. Blindsided, my mother didn't ask questions—this was many years before her own father's suicide—but rather waited for my father to elaborate on the story. They sat in the idling car for a few minutes, and then my father drove away, saying nothing more.

8.

Born in Pittsburg in 1895, my grandfather Edward White Patterson spent most of his life in Kansas. He graduated from the University of Kansas law school and practiced law before serving in Congress as the representative for Kansas's third district from 1935 to 1939. He lost a bid for third-term reelection in 1938, two years before his death. An Irishman with a fiery temper, he made a lot of devoted friends and enemies throughout his political career. In photographs from the newspaper, he stares at the camera unabashedly. There is a mixture of anger and sadness in his eyes, a kind of distance tempered only by his delicate features: high cheekbones, thin lips, small chin, and a mass of wavy hair combed up and away from his forehead.

I imagine him as amiable and charming, a man who attracted people. After his death, a colleague, described him on the House floor as "one of the finest characters and most lovable men I have served with. . . . He was always anxious to help a friend, and the influence of his upright, unselfish character will remain, as will his memory, in the hearts of the people of Kansas."

He kept promises. In his four years of service as a congressman, he was present for nearly every roll call, "honestly and sincerely trying to cast his vote for the common people." He was also a difficult and emotionally unpredictable person. I learned from the things my father left behind in his desk that Edward was a gambler and a drinker. My father believed he associated with bootleggers, many of whom operated establishments to suit those tastes.

Among the papers my mother gave me, I found the newspaper clippings related to my grandfather's death (with front-page headlines that scream "E.W. PATTERSON FATALLY SHOT") and my father's handwritten notes. The stories of his high school basketball stardom were gone. The notes, not more than a single page of text, hastily written in fragmented paragraphs, seem to outline a conversation with his sister, Patricia:

> Pat felt he killed himself—
> felt responsible because the evening before at dinner
> she refused to eat something and he had gone into a rage—
> led to an argument with Leah. Next morning Pat left for school
> without saying goodbye . . . Leah played bridge that day.
>
> In Pittsburg after losing election—mother was going to leave
> for a divorce. Father had a conversation with Pat—
> said they were going to divorce and would Patsy stay with him?
> She told him she would because she adored him—
>
> she believes that mother overheard this and subsequently said
> she would stay in the marriage for the sake of the children.

Edward was found in his car with a bullet wound to the head, at the age of forty-four. The car was in Cherokee County, with an open door, a flat tire, and two missing hubcaps, but there was no sign of an accident. Edward's body slumped toward the passenger side and his head nearly touched the floor, where a messily written suicide note fluttered near a photograph of his young son, my father. A .45 caliber automatic was clenched cold in his hand. Three empty cartridge shells lay on the floor of the car, automatically ejected from the pistol after it had been fired. No additional bullet holes were found. Yet, because the death was sudden and the empty shells raised suspicions, a coroner's inquest was called to assist with investigations at the behest of the county attorney. A coroner's jury was sworn in and taken to view the body a few hours after my grandfather was found.

My father's notes make it clear he just couldn't make *sense* of the facts of my grandfather's death. He puzzles over the fact that Edward left the house that morning with the family dog. If he planned to take his life, my father reasoned, he wouldn't have brought the dog along; this seemed incongruent with the act of committing suicide. Why did he drive to another county? Why the flat tire, the missing hubcaps? Why was the car door open when Edward was found? And why was one of his legs partially outside the vehicle? My father's notes speculate that Edward had been forced into the car at gunpoint but stubbornly left one foot on the ground. He also suggested that someone deployed the gun prior to the fatal gunshot as a warning or a threat, leaving the empty shells behind on the floor the car. Finally, he argued that an apology my grandfather made in his suicide note for his poor handwriting indicated that someone must have forced my grandfather to write it under duress.

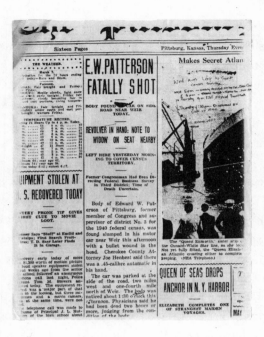

From the newspaper clippings my father left behind, I found little to suggest that Edward's death was anything other than suicide. These accounts detail a thorough investigation, conducted over several days, and the facts put into record after an inquest of multiple months, including witness testimony and reports from several physicians, all confirm suicide: "When the body was found," one part of the testimony reads, "the automatic was gripped so tightly that a clear imprint of one of the screws on the handle was firmly established in the flesh." The note found in his car was so splattered with blood it was hardly legible. "I must ask you to excuse me for the last time," it read, and spoke of wanting a simpler way out, according to one news report.

My father's theory of murder seemed thin. Still, once I had the folder of information about my grandfather in my possession, I became preoccupied with his death. For my father, and, by some extension, me, I realized Edward's death had kept us caught between two inclinations: showing and hiding the wound. Understanding Edward was one way of unlocking the mystery of my father. It seemed as if processing one death might help the other.

I started digging through public records on the internet and then in the archives of county libraries in Kansas, spending hours on the phone with several volunteer librarians. I spent hours in my study or in bed, books and papers scattered about. I read obscure histories of Pittsburg and Crawford County online. I read congressional records, law abstracts, and 1940 census material, trying to find any trace of my grandfather's work. I scoured genealogical sites and flipped through digital photo archives. Then, after one exhaustive and systematic inquiry through the archives of the Kansas Historical Society that dragged on for weeks, I discovered a collection of Edward's papers housed at Wichita State University. I was surprised to learn that the collection had been the gift of my grandmother, meticulously arranged. That she'd saved any of these materials contradicted my understanding of her efforts to erase his memory. Or was that what she had been doing by handing it all over?

I learned later, through the Center for Legislative Archives, that "most personal papers of members of Congress are geographically dispersed in repositories around the country." The two largest repositories in Kansas are the historical society in Topeka and the special collections department at Wichita State University. On the library's website, I found Edward's name among a vast number of others who had left a record of their political careers. When I dug further, I found a detailed description of *MS 75-12, Congressional Papers of E. W. Patterson.* I imagined, as I read, souvenirs wrapped in plastic sleeves, photographs sealed in wax folders, newspaper clippings neatly folded and cut. But this was just the beginning. The archive was an entry point to a search that persisted for years. And it all started with a trip to Kansas to bury my father.

9.

My mother and I arrived in Pittsburg eight days before my father's memorial service. Six months had passed since his death. Minnesota's winter had finally come to an end. The clear roads and soft ground we had been waiting for had arrived.

Pittsburg is a small town that sits on the edge of the Ozark Mountains, a mix of forest and prairie, characterized by deep, fertile soils and red clay. It's a uniquely abundant environment. And it is that abundance that granted the town what significance or prosperity it ever enjoyed: specifically, via the coal-mining industry. This began in a small way in the 1850s, when coal was hauled by wagon to Granby, Missouri, where it was used by blacksmiths. The first underground shaft in the region was sunk in 1874. By 1898, thirty mines were operating within five miles of Pittsburg, seventeen within two and half miles of town.

Broadway Street is still the main road through town today, as it was back then—a muddy dirt road with wooden sidewalks and hitching posts. Now, it's a sprawling, empty thoroughfare that shifts into a highway, boasting signs of modern development: industrial-size streetlights, strip malls, fast food restaurants, and hotels; Walmart, the Home Depot, and Starbucks gutter the north side. This is the first thing you see when you drive into town, a plateau of asphalt and parking lots. It's a town of commerce. It's a town of work.

What I knew of Pittsburg existed in fragments. I had impressionistic memories—stilled images waxed and faded, bits of rock and clay, the perfumed bathroom of my grandmother's house and the fragrance of magnolias wafting through the air. But I knew little of its history or how it might have shaped my ancestral stock. My parents left Pittsburg after they were married in the late 1950s and moved to upstate New York before settling in Minnesota. They never talked about why they'd left; they were the only members of their generations, on both sides, to leave Kansas behind. Some relatives, particularly my maternal grandmother, seemed to not only disapprove of their decision to leave Pittsburg but to view the choice as a personal affront. And so, over the years, my parents' visits home became more and more infrequent. Even as a child, I understood the journey as psychologically taxing, and I could recognize the complicated emotions aroused in sudden outbursts and arguments. On all of our visits there, my father's mood was notably volatile, his body language tense. I can still see him in the front seat of the car, clenching his teeth, the muscles at the back of his jaw throbbing in the highway's glare as my mother sat quietly in the passenger's seat.

My mother and I rented a house in town for the week. Rachel was due to fly in a few days before the funeral. My mother began organizing appointments a few hours after we had arrived and unpacked the car. The first thing on her list was a visit to the cemetery. We drove there the next morning, straight and narrow for eight miles—past a commercial strip, boarded-up buildings and empty parking lots littered with trash, the Super 8, the Sonic Drive-In, and Pittsburg State University. When we reached the gates of the Highland Park Cemetery, my mother was quick to note the irony. She and my father had lived most of their lives in the St. Paul neighborhood of the same name.

We parked the car, walked to the edge of the cemetery, and stood under a lone sycamore tree near my father's plot. Crawford and Cherokee Counties were once covered in hardwood forest: oak, hickory, sycamore, sugarberry, pecan, and honey locust, timber belts that used to thrive along the Neosho River and Cherry Creek. It was a flourishing wilderness, filled with wild game. Wolves roamed the forest in small packs and "when the sun disappeared behind the western prairies and darkness began to settle upon the earth, they came up to the cabin of the settler and howled and howled."

"It was a goodly land, fair to look upon and full of promise," Nathaniel Allison wrote in his 1904 *History of Cherokee County, Kansas and Representative Citizens*. Now, most of the trees are gone, stripped for the bounty of minerals beneath. Where the land has been remediated, much of the terrain resembles a vacant prairie, a shell of what it used to be. And where it hasn't, less than a thirty-minute drive from Pittsburg, it's a waste dump of lead-tinged dust, contaminated soil, and sinkholes.

At the cemetery, the caretaker emerged from his office and greeted us on the lawn. We followed him back inside. There, he carefully marked my father's plot on a map with an oil crayon. A red line rippled through my last name, a pointed visual representation of my patriarchal lineage. Men had been scarce in my family, and now they were all gone.

———————

My mother and I spent two more days making preparations. We had appointments with the minister, funeral director, monument service provider, and florist. Each meeting ended with a flurry of additional tasks that carried on for another couple of days, and then we were finished. Nothing to do but wait. My mother bundled up her lists, put them away, and watched television, frequently flipping channels to keep an eye on the weather, fretting over rain forecasted for the day of the memorial service.

With time on my hands and a growing feeling of restlessness, I went to the Pittsburg Public Library and resumed my search for Edward. I felt a wave of nausea as I entered the building. And yet, once I was inside, a sense of stillness washed over me.

I sat down on a bench and gazed up at the recessed fluorescent lighting in the ceiling. I closed my eyes, thinking things couldn't get any worse. It had been a long winter. Rachel had miscarried in late January. She seemed unmoored in her own grieving and I'd become wayward: sometime around then, I stopped writing. It all seemed impossible. After months of physical therapy and visits to the chiropractor, I'd regained much of my strength and was no longer in acute pain from the car accident. Now I just felt lost.

I spent most of the day in the library. I scoured old newspapers, hoping to gather more details about Edward's death; dug through genealogical materials; read historical documents and business journals relating to the early history of Pittsburg; and perused several volumes of the *Pittsburg Almanac*, an annual history published from 1876 to 1976. While my focus remained narrow—my grandfather—my search began to also widen.

In a room dedicated to Crawford County genealogy, I found a small collection of articles related to Edward's first campaign and a file that, curiously, detailed the history of his law firm, Patterson & Weir. As I skimmed through one file and then another, I kept thinking about the archive at Wichita State University. Surely, there must be something there of consequence. Wichita was only a two-hour drive from Pittsburg, and I didn't know when I'd be back in Kansas again. It made sense to make the trip. That evening, I made a rational argument to my mother, who wasn't keen about being left alone just a few days before the memorial service. When I explained to her that I'd discovered the archive, she seemed genuinely surprised. And then she said, *Yes, of course. Go.*

10.

I left early on a Wednesday. I drove straight west on Route 400, a neglected highway that begins near Joplin, Missouri, and ends in Granada, Colorado, passing through the lowlands and valleys of southern Kansas. A few miles out of Pittsburg, a small pack of coyotes trailed out of a ditch and began crossing the highway. I could see them from a distance and slowed to a stop. The pack angled in my direction, meandering across the highway, seemingly oblivious to the car's idling engine. As they passed the hood of the car, one of the animals stopped and turned to face me. It was the largest in the pack—a male, I assumed. He looked at me through the windshield, so close I could see the perimeter of his eyes, the black sheen of his nose. He was a beautiful animal: his head, muzzle, and paws strikingly red against the white of his belly and throat, his ears enormous. His eyes narrowed and then closed, as he lifted his head to sniff the air, slowly and very deliberately. When he finished, he shifted his weight from one foot to the other and flattened his ears in what looked like confusion. For a split second, I felt the impulse to turn off the car's engine and might have done so if the coyote hadn't leapt off the road and disappeared. I leaned across the passenger seat to see where he had gone, but there was no trace of him.

I opened the window and looked for the pack; they had also disappeared. All I could see was an endless field of winter wheat. It was a month before harvest and the fields were still ripening. The seeds and stalks green, florid against the limitless horizon.

My father once told me that as a young man he had often dreamed of being a farmer. He was drawn to what he perceived as a simpler life, and though he always worked hard, in his mind he simply was unable to mitigate the huge financial investment and risk he associated with farming. The closest he came to fulfilling the dream was a roughly one-acre garden he grew on a piece of property he and my mother purchased in central Minnesota when I was twelve. It was a forty-acre plot with a newly renovated, century-old Finnish homesteader's cabin, built along a river outside the small town of Menahga. Once a working farm, the land had a barn, a chicken coop, and a small hayfield, surrounded by a dense mixed forest of jack pine and spruce.

My parents and I spent nearly every weekend there, a three-hour drive from the city. They had some notion of moving there permanently once I was out of school, but my father couldn't seem to fully accept the idea of abandoning his career for a life in the country. It didn't make financial sense to him. They sold the house by the time I went to college. And yet, though the disjunction between his reality and his aspirations caused him distress, I think he enjoyed his job. At that time, he worked as a computer programmer at Sperry UNIVAC and, after more than ten years of service, was one of the company's senior managers. He had an aptitude for the mechanics of programming, often setting the standard among other employees. He was frequently called out of bed at odd hours to solve problems.

As a child, I was captivated by the idea of work and the objects related to that part of my father's life: his rack of suits and ties; his silver wide-mouthed thermos; his briefcase strewn with pens, pads of graph paper, and vanilla-colored computer cards scored with hand-written notes and computations. Once, on a visit to his office as part of a school assignment, my father gave me a tour of the computer data center, a facility that consumed an entire floor in order to hold the mainframe's numerous components and peripherals. We stood in the middle of the enormous room, dwarfed by rows of reel-to-reel units and the system's console flashing erratically with hundreds of incandescent lights, as my father explained in the most rudimentary terms what each part of the computer could do. His sheer enthusiasm about the technology was palpable as he shouted to be heard above the machinery's din.

I thought of this just outside the town of Parsons, near the site of a grain mill, the horizon glutted with rows of steel silos. Despite his dreams, it was impossible to imagine my father in any other landscape than a windowless, temperature-controlled room, crowded with machines.

At Wichita State University's special collections library, I was stripped of my pens and shoulder bag and escorted to a table where four large boxes had been arranged. I was given several loose sheets of paper, three pencils, and a pair of paper gloves. *For fragile items—they should be clearly marked*, the librarian said.

Among folders of newspaper clippings, campaign propaganda, and paper souvenirs, there were only a handful of photographs. I found them in an envelope in the last box. As I removed them one by one from a shroud of protective vellum and arranged them on the table, these portraits seemed to create a world, an indestructible record of the past. The fact that I had never seen any of these pictures gave me the sensation that I was meeting not just Edward for the first time but also my father, as though a part of each of them was only beginning to exist.

In one photo, my grandparents stand together among a row of newly elected congressmen. In the background: an ornately framed mirror and an American flag. Leah, my grandmother, leans against my grandfather's arm, a small purse hooked over her elbow. The occasion is formal. She wears white gloves and a matching pillbox hat, a mink stole draped over her shoulders. Edward tilts slightly to one side, a faint smile progressing across his face. Though he looks uncomfortable posing for the camera, he exudes an unmistakable charisma that draws my attention, an almost physical presence that gives me a vaguely unrequited feeling. The resemblance to my father is striking.

In another photo, he stands beside a plane in an arid field. The struts and bay of the plane's upper wing rise behind him and a dozen or so other men, all standing in a row, crowded together on the airfield. Two years since his first election and the next on the horizon. In another, he stands next to his mother, years before. The same light splits a grove of trees in a park. Branches grow dark and lose their arms in his head. And in another, Leah, seated in his lap, lightly touches his neck. Her expression is sullen, serious. And then they are standing together on an open lawn, my grandfather dressed in a military uniform. Under the crisp pockets of a tunic, a garrison cap hangs over an empty pistol strap like a skinned fowl.

I studied these images carefully and then moved on to the other boxes, sifting first through a collection of campaign literature, calling cards, buttons: ephemera brought back from Washington. I opened formal invitations to congressional dinners, presidential luncheons, Democratic fundraising events, and inaugural balls. I found handwritten thank-you notes from President Franklin Delano Roosevelt, transcripts of speeches and radio broadcasts, and one handmade birthday card my father created as a child, all of which my grandmother had saved over the years—a weird mix of history and memorabilia.

In the last box, there were more than two hundred newspaper articles tracing the arc of my grandfather's political career. Everything was there except news of his death. At first, I was disappointed, but as I began to read, my preoccupation with his suicide temporarily faded and I found myself absorbing every smallest detail of my grandfather's political life, information that had previously been eclipsed—or erased—by his death.

I read stories of him bursting into town hall meetings with union members as a form of protest; picketing alongside others; passing out dollar bills to striking workers; bringing people to tears with campaign speeches and receiving standing ovations in filled auditoriums. I knew these histories were littered with omissions. As they were largely published in partisan sources—union-hall newsletters and party-line newspapers—I felt sure their portrait of my grandfather's political character had been inflated. I read with skepticism, with an eye toward the heated rhetoric of that era: of whiteness, national pride, and tradition. But I also read with excitement, with eagerness to meet a man I never knew.

"Red-headed, fearless and full of fight," as one article described him, on the floor of Congress Edward was nicknamed the "Fighting Irishman from the Balkans." (The district my grandfather represented was often called the "Little Balkans," in reference both to the large number of European immigrants—including Italians, Bulgarians, Serbians, and Croatians—who'd come to work the mines and to the Balkan-like turmoil created by the fractious history between coal-company management and the unions.) As a politician, my grandfather fought hard for workers' rights. A social liberal and lifelong Democrat, he was a fierce supporter of labor and an advocate for social justice. His writings often evince anti-capitalist sentiments and calls to redistribute wealth and power, revealing a streak of populism, which later on would put him in political alliance with socialists. In his first run for office, in the midst of one of the worst years in the Great Depression, he campaigned on behalf of living wages and fair profits, controlled currency inflation, and the repeal of Prohibition and governmental waste. He criticized Herbert Hoover's public works projects as wasteful government spending and his local relief programs as a "callous disregard for the unemployed."

Why had my father never mentioned any of this? How was it that I knew so little of my ancestral history?

Later, I'd learn that Crawford County—like many other places—was very poor in the 1930s. The market for coal had collapsed. The 1930 Federal Unemployment Census found a general unemployment rate of 3.2 percent, but for coal miners the figure was 20.8 percent. By November 1931, the mining industries of Crawford and

Cherokee Counties had the worst employment conditions in all of Kansas. Visits from representatives from the Governor's Committee for Employment to various parts of Crawford County confirmed that "children were wrapped in newspapers" during the winter months to stay warm. Even while local businesses and organizations donated bread, milk, and meat to needy families, many survived by bootlegging. "The liquor traffic has very evidently been the means of keeping most of these families alive," read the report. "Farmers cannot leave home without their chickens and food being stolen."

My father was born in August 1931 as my grandfather entered his first, unsuccessful race for Congress at the age of thirty-six. I imagine the day sweltering in heat. His mother laboring long under the dull lights of the hospital as his father paced the floor in the waiting room, perhaps nursing liquor from a flask concealed in his breast pocket. In a letter written one week following my father's birth, Leah's father, William Kennedy, proudly announced, *I am thrilled through and through over your darling little boy. I am so glad it is a boy. I am further thrilled with the name between the historic names of James the 1st and Patterson. . . . It is fine to have the name Kennedy carried along down the centuries long after I am with that long galaxy of men who wrap the drapery of their couch about them and lie down to pleasant dreams.*

When he ran again several years later, my grandfather was inspired by Roosevelt's 1932 landslide election and his vision to redefine the responsibility of the federal government, a responsibility for social welfare. My grandfather lauded these ideas as pragmatic, not ideological, and promised in his campaign that if elected he would vote in favor of Roosevelt's reforms, that he would vote for the "economic security of the people of the nation." It was a strategy that paid off. In 1934, when my grandfather was finally elected, the third district hadn't elected a Democrat in over thirty years. Once in office, my grandfather became a New Deal Democrat, championing Roosevelt's initiatives and programs, the foundations of which had been laid in the president's first hundred days. The speed of governmental change then, as many have written, was enormous. From 1933 to 1935, writes Louis Menand in an article in the *New Yorker*, the Seventy-Third Congress "restored the banking system, increased federal unemployment assistance to the states, asserted the right of workers to organize, and gave the federal government the power to oversee production and prices in some industries."

The Seventy-Fourth Congress—of which my grandfather was a member—passed the Social Security Act; the Wagner Act, which promoted labor unions; and the Robinson-Patman Act of 1936, which fixed minimum retail prices on products to prevent suppliers and manufacturers from offering better prices to larger chain stores over smaller shops. A promise of recovery and reform to bring an end to the Great Depression, the New Deal was made possible by a one-party rule of Democrats, a fact my grandfather often cited in his political speeches. But while the New Deal helped many who were suffering from the events of the Depression, within the Democratic Party and the policy's narrative of progress, there remained a scourge.

New Deal policy relied on the support of Southern Democrats to succeed. While economically progressive, these politicians used their power to fight for policies that upheld white supremacy. Southern Democrats wouldn't vote for the New Deal if it included desegregation, and so Roosevelt allowed them to profoundly shape the legislation. As Menand notes, they made changes in bills regulating minimum wage to the exclusion of domestic and agriculture workers, jobs largely held by Black Americans; impeded anti-lynching legislation; and "exercised strict control over how and to whom [New Deal] money trickled down in their states," further cementing regional and racial disparities, and creating a system of division that endures today.

Like Roosevelt, my grandfather stayed away from the subject of segregation, though he also seems to have made a point of separating himself from Southern Democrats, and in his writing and speeches frequently championed the cause of "human rights." Many inside the Kansas Democratic Party criticized him for being too progressive. And he drew ire from conservatives for his "socialist" policies. I found a number of references citing verbal attacks from both his political opponents and his allies.

In the library I read for hours, taking careful notes. I wanted as little as possible to be lost to memory. I wanted a tangible record of the archive that I would soon have to leave behind. I knew in the moment that I was unburying a history that had been unnecessarily buried, but I didn't yet fully appreciate what it meant to in some way bring Edward to life. Years later, after I understood more about the history of the region and of Pittsburg itself, I could trace what I imagined to be his path to progressive politics and could even see myself in his expressed idealism, helping me to understand how this mercurial man had shaped my life. But on that day in the library, I kept circling back to his death. I believed Edward's suicide was intricately connected to my father's. I had a ruminative need to make sense of these deaths—to imagine, in the most accurate way, the last day of Edward's life, a story that might somehow inform my future. Or, better yet, inoculate it.

11.

March 6, 1940, a Wednesday. My grandfather prepares
to leave for what he says will be a two-day business trip.
It's a cold morning. A thin veil of frost behind the drawn
bedroom curtains begins to melt as he stands in front
of a mirror, adjusting his tie. From a dressing table he
removes a gold-plated wristwatch. It's 11:30 a.m.

As my grandfather finishes packing the remainder of
his bag and cinching the leather straps tight, he glances at
the bed's cherry headboard, rising above a row of decorative ticking pillows. Four months have passed since his move
back to Pittsburg after an unsuccessful bid for a third-term
reelection. He hasn't lived here in years, but the house and
furnishings are still familiar. He leans into the furniture now,
running his hand over a pink satin bedspread, and then lies
down face-first, drawing in the bed's scent. Minutes pass as
he closes his eyes, drifting momentarily away.

I imagine my grandmother in the kitchen, scouring
a skillet. She's angry. From scraps of evidence in my
father's notes, I know she and my grandfather are in the
midst of a lingering argument, which began last night
at dinner, when my aunt Patricia left the table before
she was excused, ignoring her buttered carrots.

—*Goddamn it!* he'd said, pounding his fist on the table,
as Patricia slid out of her chair and away.

—*Don't*, my grandmother said, reaching toward him.

—*She's going to eat everything on her plate*, he replied, rising from his seat. *I mean it!*

As he stood, his arm swept the table, bringing his plate and half-full glass of whiskey to the floor. Shards scattered and liquor pooled at my grandfather's feet as my aunt ran up the stairs to her bedroom.

—*Get back here right now!*

My father sat silently at the table, pushing his fork across an empty plate. My grandmother stood and gently stroked his head.

—*Go to your room*, she told him.

—*Jesus fucking Christ—we're not finished*, my grandfather screamed, retrieving more liquor from a buffet. He stood in the center of the room, the neck of the bottle pinched between his fingers.

My father left the table quickly, put his plate on the counter in the kitchen, and then ran to his bedroom, where he listened to arguments swell into the night.

Now the children are away at school. They slipped out this morning without saying goodbye. My grandmother rinses the skillet in a bath of hot water, and a faint curtain of steam rises before her face.

Close to his head, my grandfather can hear the ticking of his watch, and in the distance, the clang of iron against the kitchen sink. He opens his eyes and inches his arm closer to the pillow, where he blindly feels for his pistol. He's been sleeping with a gun for years. When he finds it, he pulls it forward and above his head, fingering the rosewood grip with his thumb, feeling the weight of it, flat against his palm. He checks the grip safety, then tucks the gun in the high waist of his pants. Now he's up, ready to whistle for the family's Airedale terrier. The dog, asleep near the front door, wakes before my grandfather has emitted a sound, bounding up to meet him at the head of the stairs. He tugs at the dog's ear, then waves toward the door. The dog runs ahead, waiting at the threshold, as my grandfather calls out into the house.

—*I'm leaving now*, he says.

My grandmother is still in the kitchen washing dishes.

—*All right*, she says, with a tone of indifference.

My grandfather removes his coat from a small closet. He shakes it vigorously and slips it on as he passes through the open door, the dog tangled in his feet with excitement.

It's almost noon. Through the windshield of the car, still wet from the morning's frost, my grandfather looks up to the sky, a blue horizon above the brick chimney of the house.

Inside, my grandmother leaves the kitchen and moves upstairs to retrieve laundry from a bedroom closet. As she passes the window, she stops to notice her husband in the front seat of the idling car. He appears to be looking up at her, but as she parts the curtain to widen her view, she realizes his gaze is skyward. She looks up, too, though she sees nothing more than the bare branches of a tree. The dog notices her then and begins to bark, standing erect on the seat. My grandfather turns to the dog, forcing him down with one hand on the animal's rump, then pulls the car into gear and backs out of the driveway.

He drives the full length of Winwood Drive, then turns right at Catalpa. Driving past Lakeside Park, he turns first on Washington and then down Broadway. The sun above floods the street in an onslaught of light, casting everything in a haze: Harry's Cafe, the Colonial Theatre, and the Bee Hive Cafe, where a group of men loiter outside. As my grandfather passes, he tips the car's sun visor forward and then, recognizing a friend, taps the horn, raising a hand in a stagnant wave. He drives a few more blocks down Broadway, turns on Ninth Street, and pulls over to the curb one block west, at Pine. He lingers only for a few seconds in front of his childhood home, then continues on, turning south to follow Walnut to Jefferson, before circling back to Broadway, passing his sister's house, a stately white building with Tuscan columns and heavy carved balusters, on the way. He slows the car for a moment, easing his foot off the gas for a few seconds, and then quickly accelerates, driving south to the end of Broadway. As he turns right onto Route 69, a pheasant explodes from a ditch, careening toward the car's windshield. My grandfather swerves as the bird sweeps the hood and disappears, dropping into a cornfield. The dog barks hysterically. My grandfather rights the car back onto the road and speeds on.

By 12:30 p.m., he arrives in Cherokee, a small town—once a mining camp—now in slow economic decline. He has lunch at Idle-A-While Bar and Grill. He orders coffee and a veal potpie, with peach meringue for dessert. Later, he's at a blind pig down the street, drinking highballs with Walter Cook in an empty windowless room behind the facade of an ice cream parlor. Walter is one of this year's census takers in the district. My grandfather's mind is still on politics, and as this census is the first to poll people door to door, he wants to listen carefully to the enumerators, hoping he might hear a story that will illuminate his own fight for Roosevelt's New Deal. Democrats across the country have lost their seats in the midterms, in part a reaction to the country's sharp economic downturn, and many initiatives of the New Deal are under threat. But after a few drinks, Walter doesn't seem too interested in talking business. Their conversation drifts. Impatient, my grandfather swallows the last of his drink and gets up to leave the bar.

The sun, beginning its descent in the west, is less invasive than before as my grandfather slips out the back door into the alley, making his way back to his car. Still, he feels the pleasure of its heat. Without reason, as he walks, he's thinking of the pheasant, the bird's short wings and bladelike tail slurring his mind like a fetish. He remembers the stories his father once told about his days in Deadwood, South Dakota, and the birds he'd shot and dressed in fields to carry to his gold-digging claim in the hills. *Easier to skin a pheasant than a rabbit*, he'd said, *and they taste better too—a discernible flavor of apple.*

Thinking of his father now, his mood begins to shift. When my grandfather was just a boy, his father's health broke and slowly declined. When thinking of his father now, he can't help but touch sadness. In the front seat of the car, he sits with the dog's head cradled in his lap. His attention heightens, even as his senses begin to dull. What he thinks are hours are actually only minutes, and when he finally checks his watch, he begins to weep, watching people pass by in the street. Disturbed by these feelings, he thinks to clear his head with a drive. He follows the railroad bed east of town, past the strip pits and then back, taking more than an hour, before he finally turns left on a gravel road, Northeast Tenth Street, driving until he nearly meets the highway. He stops here, near an intersection and a barren field. Dusk. He steps out of the car and the dog follows.

—*Go*, he says.

The dog bolts into the field and my grandfather watches him run. In the distance, a coal-mining tipple and the swinging crane of a power shovel gleam in a cloud of smoke from the zinc smelters. And to the east, behind a grove of trees, a row of headstones in the Hosey Hill Cemetery that my grandfather can't see. He walks to the back of the car, glancing again at the field to see the dog leaping through the blue-stemmed scrub. Now, as he leans back against the slope of the car's back end, he withdraws the gun, flexing his hand over the pistol's handle and sliding his feet into the gravel, as though stretching into sand. Removing the magazine, he sets the gun down on the trunk of the car, fingering the ammunition bound at the top, then the subtle movement of the magazine's spring and each hole in the magazine's side, filled with the bright brass of the bullets' casings. He turns the clip, the sheen flaring in the descending light.

Next, he loads the magazine and slides open the safety. He walks a few steps away from the car, down the center of the road. The dog bounds out of the field and begins to trail him, panting wildly. My grandfather has imagined the darkness soon to come many times before—always with a sense of relief. He calls the dog back into the car, nipping a little whiskey from a bottle he keeps in the trunk.

He composes a note to my grandmother on the back of a census form found in the bag he'd packed that morning, holding the page against the edge of the steering wheel as he writes. When he's finished, he begins thinking of the ammunition stacked in his hand, the top round waiting for release. He imagines the face of the slide pushing the bullet into the chamber, the slide forcing the barrel forward, the squeeze of the trigger. He sees the firing pin's strike igniting, the bullet pushed through the barrel, and then the brass casing tearing out of the ejection port.

Now he rests the gun in his lap and robs the contents of his wallet to find a picture of his son. He weeps again, dropping it to the floor.

He rolls down the window of the car, pushes the dog to the floor, and fires the gun. The sound of the shot is deafening. The dog whines as the bullet's casing ricochets off the ceiling and onto the seat. My grandfather opens the door and lets the animal out. He fires again.

Then he closes the window and fires one last shot.

In the early afternoon of March 7, Lewey Jones is hauling coal in the back of a company flatbed, driving south on the gravel road where Edward's black Ford coupe has been parked through the night. Edward's dog begins barking wildly as Jones pulls the truck to the left, trying to avoid the dog as he approaches the car. He leans over to the passenger window, pausing only long enough to clearly see the body slumped inside, a wave of anxiety

expelling a faint sound from his mouth, *Mercy* shaping
between his teeth. Soon he's speeding east toward the
town of Weir to find the sheriff.

Leah is at her weekly bridge game, in a living room
flooded with sunlight. The game is moving slowly, with her
opponents' team fighting for every last possible advantage.
She's just won the trick with a dummy trump, leaving her
side a few points away from a grand slam. In her mind, the
game is already won.

Elsewhere, a police car idles outside of Leah's house.
One officer knocks on the door, using the end of a night-
stick, trying to rouse anyone inside, while another walks
through the yard, tapping on windows, checking locks.
No one is home; the house is empty.

The sun begins to drop behind a grove of oak trees
at the side of a gravel road. It's noticeably cooler now
than only a few hours ago, and a damp chill rises from
the field. The medical examiner, Samuel Muller, stands
at the back end of my grandfather's car. Through the
rear window, he can see a trace of my grandfather's left
shoulder pitched above the seat. The sheriff waves him
forward. Muller slips on examination gloves, his hands
held high above his waist, exhaust from a nearby police
car lifting into the cool air. He walks toward the front of
the car, fingers absently tracing the metal. Smooth, cold,
clean. He thinks of the last person he examined, a death
by natural causes, a diversion from the blood he now begins to see on the glass and interior of the car.

It's almost 4:00 p.m. when Leah, escorted by two
police officers, arrives at the scene. Muller has already
finished his initial examination, and Lee Best, Cherokee

County's acting coroner and a good friend of my grand-father's, has arrived, ordering that the body be removed from the scene. At his direction, it's taken to the Naylor Funeral Home in Weir, where a further examination will be made.

As the police car carrying Leah approaches the empty car on the gravel road, she looks out the window. She is still wearing the pearls and pillbox hat, the black suede shoes. She begins to feel odd about her choice of attire, aware that, in a moment, she must step outside the confines of this space and be a widow. She's still considering this when Lee Best's face appears in the window. Though his expression is grim, he some-how manages to smile, which puts her momentarily at ease. He opens the door and helps my grandmother out of the car.

—*I'm so very sorry*, he says. *They've found a note—I thought you'd want to see it. I've made arrangements for you to sit in my car. You'll have more privacy.*

Referenced in one newspaper account as the "out-standing evidence of suicide," the note is seized by investigators after my grandmother reads it and is entered into a body of evidence submitted to the coro-ner's inquest.

———

Ten days after my grandfather's death, the inquest con-vened in the back room of the funeral home in Weir: testimony, muttered evidence, a vivid description of the bullet's path as delivered by Muller, who also told of the condition of the body when it was found. Facts previously discovered in the investigation were put into the record by a Cherokee County district court reporter. Frank and Bill White, who lived near Weir, testified that they had seen my grandfather's car stopped on the side of the road nearly twenty hours before the body was discovered. They made two trips past the vehicle, they said. The first time the car door was closed and the second time it was open. The right rear tire was flat. There was cash remaining in my grandfather's pockets, and his watch, still on his wrist, was running. His dog was waiting outside the car. Witnesses included my grandfather's brother-in-law, who identified the body after it was found "on a lonely road west of Weir," as one newspaper reported.

The inquest was officially closed by early May. No new evidence was entered into the record. The coroner's report, made official a few days later, included a list of personal property found on the body: *One 45 Cal. pistol, a billfold containing $16.00 currency, Elks & V.F.W. membership cards, driver's license, black notebook, pen & pencil set, V.F.W. Insignia, tie, garage key, Hamilton wrist watch, $2.45 in coins, farewell note, and one bottle of Old Grand-Dad Whiskey.*

The above property was on the 10th day of May 1940, given to the deceased widow, Leah Patterson, the last paragraph of the report reads, *with the exception of the whiskey, which was confiscated by Clarence Burger, Sheriff.*

My grandfather was buried on March 23. His funeral was held at the Presbyterian Church in Pittsburg. Hundreds of people attended. Mrs. Staneart Graham sang "In the City Foursquare," and as the casket was carried out of the church, Mrs. Hallman played "Nearer My God to Thee" on the church organ. Following the services, the body was taken to Kansas City for cremation.

Last Tribute
The Frontenac Times
March 15, 1940

Democrats lost a champion last Thursday in the death of Edward White Patterson, Third District census supervisor and former member of Congress.

Mr. Patterson, whose body was found fatally shot in his car two miles west of and one-half mile north of Weir, was well-known and well liked in Frontenac and throughout the country. He always said, "Next to Pittsburg, I would make Frontenac my home."

He was a man who continually looked out for Frontenac. When he was in Congress he helped to secure the federal aid for our city; and without his untiring efforts, we would never have been able to get a WPA project in laying more than eight miles of water pipe here. He was also a great aid in securing a federal fish hatchery at Farlington Lake.

Mr. Patterson always had a warm spot deep down in his heart for the common people. Up until his very death, he always fought for the rights of the common laborer, the unemployed, and the WPA worker. Mr. Patterson was also a friend of organized labor. Each time he ran for public office, he was endorsed by all trade unions.

At this hour of bereavement, we wish to console his family, whom Mr. Patterson loved so dearly.

Last Tribute
Oswego Democrat
March 13, 1940

In the death of Edward Patterson Oswego lost one of the best political friends it ever had— the only real congressman who ever kept his word with our people when he promised to secure a post office for our city.

When he promised to do all in his power to secure the beautiful building we now have he did not promise to give it to us at once but said, "you can depend upon me doing everything in my power to secure the appropriation just as soon as possible." And he did as he promised.

The Oswego post office will stand as a monument to the fidelity of Ed Patterson, a man who kept his word. Peace to his troubled soul and the gratitude of this community.

12.

I've read the notes my father kept about Edward's death many times over the years. Each time I read them, I can see my father searching for a way to understand the events of his past as well as a father he barely knew. Each time, I look for a motive, a theory, but what I see is suspicion and circumstantial evidence.

The foundation of my father's belief that Edward was murdered, as I have said, lay in the odder details surrounding his death. The empty bullet casings, the flat tire, the missing hubcaps, the illegible handwriting of the suicide note. In his notes, he asks, again and again, questions that he felt pointed to murder:

> He drove to Cherokee County because the coroner there was a friend?

> He explained the handwriting because he knew that it would be questioned for its illegibility—?

Then there was the inquest, which, he wrote, *found the cause of death was "person or persons unknown."* I'm not sure how my father came to this conclusion. In one of the articles in my father's files, Cherokee County Attorney Joe Henbest is quoted as saying, "There are indications of suicide, but we are not sure yet that it was." But in all of my research, I've never found any source that uses the language my father did.

SUICIDE NOTE LEFT

PATTERSON APPARENTLY SHOT SELF.

Identify Handwriting and Pistol As Belonging To the Prominent Kansas Politician; No Motive Yet Discovered.

A note written to his wife by E. W. Patterson of Pittsburg, former member of Congress and supervisor of district No. 3 for the 1940 federal census was the outstanding evidence indicating Patterson had committed suicide sometime early yesterday, investigating authorities reported.

Why an inquest at all? My father may have thought the pursuit of one proved Edward's death suspicious, but it was really a matter of routine. When a person dies or a human body is found in Kansas, and when the death is suspected to have been the result of violence, whether by unlawful means or by suicide, the county coroner decides if an investigation should take place. The Cherokee County coroner was my grandfather's friend. It's obvious that he would have followed the law and probable he would have done his due diligence for Edward. Furthermore, I confirmed in at least one newspaper account that "no information was brought out in the hearing that had not been anticipated," that the "county attorney had said that the death from a pistol bullet wound through the head appeared to be suicide." And while any transcript of a coroner's inquest has since been destroyed per standard policy, I was later able to find a copy of the coroner's report—which lists suicide as the cause of death.

———

Alcoholic—could not stop, the first sentence of my father's notes reads, floating in a gully of white space. Then, abruptly, a second, composed like a headline:

> Politician—Refused at Gun Point to
> join the Ku Klux Klan—
> KKK against Catholics!!

This is followed by his brief explanation of the Ku Klux Klan's virulent opposition to Catholics in the region. *More than Blacks—not so many in Pittsburg then*, he scribbles. *Later the ballots stuffed against him as County Attorney.*

I first thought of this note—the dramatic refusal, the explanation of relative prejudices, and the accusations of ballot stuffing—as crude exaggeration, but after some research, I wasn't so sure. The Klan *did* have a big presence in southeastern Kansas in the 1920s, a part of the Klan's second rise nationwide. In fact, by the time my grandfather made a bid for county attorney in 1924, Pittsburg's chapter boasted more than four thousand members, the largest in the state. Outside of town, a cross burned in a baseball field where Klan members met for rallies and barbecues. As in many parts of rural America, the region included several sundown towns, though the primary focus for the Klan, at least within the confines of Pittsburg, was on running Catholics out of positions of power. As historian Kathleen Belew notes, the second Klan "drew white Protestants, opportunistically capitalizing on local tensions in multiple regions throughout the county." In southeastern Kansas, specifically, historian James N. Leiker writes, "Preachers often welcomed into Sunday services robed Klansmen who marched down center aisle, handed over packets of cash, and legitimized their roles as militant Christians equally prone to charity and strength." Anti-Catholicism was an existing political stance in Kansas, an easy platform for the Klan to exploit.

Outside the halls of church, the Klan gained recruits among those who were upset by the region's increase in "crime and anarchy," appealing to culturally conservative farmers, business owners, and others who feared their livelihoods were threatened by the "lawless spirit" of the mining towns, largely attributed to immigrant (that is, mostly Catholic) workers. One Oklahoman newspaper described the region as "over-run with the worst cut throats, murderers and all-around criminals that ever disgraced a civilized county."

As the Klan's popularity swelled, the organization made efforts to draw the attention of Crawford County politicians. At an outdoors Klan meeting in 1924, supporters gathered before an enormous electric cross draped with an American flag as Mart Montee, then mayor of Pittsburg, announced a bid for governor, asking for the Klan's support. He was joined by the pastor of Pittsburg's United Brethren Church, campaigning for the third-district seat in Congress—the same seat my grandfather would later hold—on the Klan's Citizen ticket.

It's easy to imagine, then, the Klan attempting to persuade my grandfather, as he ran for county attorney, to become another candidate for their party, in an effort to present a Klan-endorsed slate of candidates in the general election. Instead, however, they endorsed A. H. Carl, my grandfather's opponent, who ran on a campaign of eliminating bootlegging in the county. And the ballot stuffing? Who can say? But my grandfather *was* defeated, losing to Carl, before eventually winning the county attorney position two years later.

This is the second fundamental part of my father's belief: Edward had made a lot of enemies. *Would never sit in front of an open window*, he writes next in his notes. *Always had the shades drawn.*

And it wasn't just the Ku Klux Klan. It was the mob too. According to my mother—this is paratext; my father doesn't mention it in his notes—my father had focused on Edward's association with David Joseph "Papa Joe" Saia, one of the most famous politicians in southeastern Kansas. Saia was born in Chicopee, a Sicilian camp near Pittsburg that Leiker asserts had an "active chapter of the Black Hand," a group he describes as a "predecessor to the mafia" (though this assertion is hard to verify).

Saia was a big-hearted man with a "loud, gravelly voice who made sausage, wine and meatballs—and always had a steady flow of people coming and going around him." He was the first person of Italian descent to win office in Crawford County and served as county commissioner for more than fifty years. Forced to quit school and go to work in the coal mines at age thirteen, he became an active union member, committed to workers' rights and political causes. He believed, according to one interview, that the poor working conditions of the mines had pushed him into politics, as this was the best way for him to advance economically and socially without much formal education. He was elected precinct party leader and became vice chair of the Crawford County Democratic Central Committee in 1934, when he was thirty years old. He quickly rose in the Democratic Party ranks from there.

Unsurprisingly, given their shared sympathies, Saia and my grandfather were staunch political allies. (My father maintained, incorrectly, that Saia had also formerly been my grandfather's law partner.) Once elected, Edward appointed Saia relief supervisor to the Works Progress Administration (WPA), a decision that was out of step with traditional political culture—most WPA relief jobs were distributed through political machines. Saia was quickly fired by party leaders in Pittsburg. My grandfather defiantly reinstated him, but they only fired Saia again. Later, Saia expressed his discontent with the WPA hiring system, stating, "I am bitterly opposed to any system that makes provisions to take care of half the needy while the other half literally starve to death." Disenchanted with politics, Saia quit his WPA efforts and started work in the Farmer-Labor Union, organized to represent relief workers and the unemployed. The union, which eventually flourished statewide with Saia as its first president, was, in Crawford County, composed mainly of former coal miners and farmers who'd lost their farms during the Depression.

But my father also suspected that, through Saia, Edward was linked to the mob. And he thought that Saia had introduced Edward to business in the mob that eventually got him killed, although my father never articulated the specifics of what that business or his trespass might have been.

Did the mob even exist in the area? The Black Hand, note historians Patrick G. O'Brien, Kenneth J. Peak, and Barbara K. Robins, "extorted money from its victims with dire threats" in the mining towns, where "violent acts were committed in its name," but there's no verifiable connection between these groups and the mafia, despite what residents of the region have sometimes claimed. Pittsburg journalist J. T. Knoll describes the region's Black Hand as "local tough guys who did stuff, but not like the big-time mob." Still, the rumors fly. When I did a Google search for Joe Saia and the town of Frontenac, the bootlegging hub where he lived, I found a few outlandish stories on message board threads, which Knoll says are "all fantasyland." Knoll says he has never found any evidence to connect Joe Saia to the mob or to any groups active in organized crime. He describes Saia as a "master politician who would go out of his way to help a person in need." He was perhaps a bit of a "rough and tumble guy," who relied—as many did in those days—on a system of patronage to succeed. But, Knoll says, there was nothing criminal about him.

———————

To learn more about the history of the mob in the region and to confirm my doubts regarding my father's theory, I contacted a local historian on a later trip to Kansas. A trim man with a broad face, Jerry Lomshek has lived his entire life in Chicopee. With his full head of silver hair and long sideburns, he looks just like his Slovenian ancestors might have when they arrived in the area.

On the day I visited his house, he walked me through a room containing a wall-sized card catalog that he'd salvaged from a library. The cabinet was stuffed with Lomshek's encyclopedic notes, filled with a variety of information including oral histories, article citations, and newspaper references. In preparation for my arrival, he had already pulled out a drawer that held a few cards for my grandfather. He told me he had a card for every prominent citizen of Pittsburg.

    —Of course, your grandfather was very well known, he said.

His catalog didn't offer me anything new, but it helped me think through the circumstances of Edward's death. I showed him the newspaper clippings I'd collected, carefully explaining the details my father had questioned.

Lomshek listened carefully, nodding occasionally as he shuffled through the clippings. Then he began to respond. While some of the details did seem odd, he agreed, he was skeptical that my grandfather had been murdered. For one thing, Lomshek said, most mafia killings in rural outposts were designed to leave no trace. If the murder was intended to be more visible, then my grandfather would have likely been killed execution style, with a shot to the back of the head or mowed down by a gang with machine guns. Why would the mob go to the trouble of staging a suicide? They had no reason to be so calculating, Lomshek explained. And if the killing were meant to be symbolic, as my father had believed, the gestures would have been far more brutal. Men killed to send a message were often tortured or beaten first. Or strangled, then stuffed into barrels. Or dismembered and thrown into a river. Or found in the trunk of a car with a dime on their chests. Or with a canary stuffed in their mouths.

    —In those days, around here, if they wanted you gone—you simply disappeared, he said. *There's a lot of empty land and the night is long.*

    —So they buried bodies? I asked.

—That's right—there's makeshift graves all over. There's a lot of unsolved murder cases in Crawford County alone, most of which happened during the state's prohibition, when crime got organized.

So why did my father believe in his theory of murder, however untenable some of its conjectures might have been? The violence and disruption of his past, maybe, growing up in the shadows of Prohibition, the Great Depression, and the historically violent and chaotic culture of Crawford County. But more, I think, because believing Edward was murdered would have made it easier to avoid the questions a loss by suicide presents.

He wasn't the only one who avoided the subject. After Edward's death, my grandmother Leah did everything she could to put him behind her. In the weeks following the funeral, as she sorted through business affairs and began coping with the reality of supporting a family, she stopped talking about her husband. What happens, I wondered, to a child whose father literally and figuratively disappears?

One final sentence near the bottom of my father's notes leaps out from the page. *Father had a conversation with Pat—said they were going to divorce and would Patsy stay with him*: but this isn't the sentence I mean. To the left of the word *Father*, circled in red ink, there's a question written in the margin— *What do I call him?*—circled again with the same red ink.

The question cuts sharp. As if Edward, as a father, was capricious, removed. Or, more precisely, a mystery.

13.

My first relative arrived in Pittsburg in 1882. William Lemuel Patterson, my great-grandfather, jostled southward on a train from Iowa. He was Midwestern born and bred, raised in an upper-class home, but had a pioneer's restlessness. While higher education had been a part of most of his ancestors' lives, he hadn't taken as much formal schooling as his parents desired. Instead, new frontiers and money beckoned. It's a pattern I traced throughout the Patterson line. From one generation to the next—men following a reckless path of wealth through legitimate and illegitimate means. They were lawyers, bankers, and politicians, but they were also gamblers, gold-diggers, and salesmen.

My great-grandfather went west for a few years first. I have a copy of the diary he kept for exactly thirteen months in 1877, when he staked a claim in Deadwood, South Dakota, at the age of twenty-one. Prospecting in the Black Hills back then was a young man's game, and when reading his diary entries, I get the feeling of being at the beginning of something—I hear the voice of a man who wants to take a risk, to gamble, to get his hands dirty. I can also hear that he's fallen under the spell of the frontier (a word that originally meant "boundary," but over time slipped into usage as an adjective, a noun, an

American myth). He had the privilege and the means—more or less—to adventure, to fail, to be an iconoclast. Reading his diary, however, you'd have the impression that his economic future depended on striking it rich. *We have now been at work on our claim, just two weeks and have for somewhat near 25 cents each, but when we didn't [sic] our expenses for grub and pick and sharpening, we are out less than fourteen dollars apiece. This must pan out better than that again Saturday or this child starts for Fort Pier,* he writes.

Even though he was young, he was already showing signs of physical weakness. Many days, he made the "sick list" and was left behind in the camp to *make some mush and keep the fires red hot.* And the claim he and his companions—Hank, Eli, and Custer—made never paid off. Over several months in the winter, they struck many pits in the hills, stripping and sluicing in snow, without much profit. By late April, the men had given up. They walked to Deadwood, looking for work, and when that didn't succeed, they left on a train for Fort Pierre. There, they sold their firearms for thirty-one dollars to *some Pilgrims who think they are going to make their fortunes in the hills.* On May 9, 1877, my great-grandfather wrote his last diary entry: *We have made arrangements with a carpenter to make us a boat for fourteen dollars to be done in the morning by five o'clock, if the steam boat doesn't make its appearance before that time. We expect to be four days in getting to Yankton some three hundred and forty miles. And of our readers who want to follow us through our hardships and trials will find us in our Last Addition—Down the Missouri.*

He returned home and, with the help of his father, a successful barrister, opened a shoe store in the town of Scandia in north Kansas. It seems to have been a good life. By then, William had been courting Ida White, from Ainsworth, Iowa, for several years. She was a petite, beautiful woman, who made the most intoxicating jellies he'd ever tasted. He was waiting until he amassed enough money to propose—but then a tornado flattened his store. An empty slate. His ambitions fixed on the vast new America unfolding elsewhere in the heart of the country. He'd heard stories of booming coal towns springing up all over eastern Kansas and Missouri. He smelled money. He promised Ida he'd return for her and got back on the train.

He got off in Joplin. He spent a few days there but saw no prospects. One of the first towns in the region to secure a passenger rail line, Joplin was already a thriving metropolis, cluttered with mercantile. Just over the state line in Kansas, though, he had heard a town named Pittsburg was just beginning to take shape under a booming coal industry.

"Pittsburg, for miles around, is underlaid with an inexhaustible supply of high grade bituminous coal," a 1890 pamphlet aimed at attracting manufacturers affirmed. "Imagine a train of cars leading in a continuous line from Pittsburg to New York, each car loaded with 80,000 pounds of coal, and you have an idea of the enormous output of the mines in this district. . . . Pittsburg has no fear of famine or shortage for years to come. . . . She may fearlessly go on building and manufacturing as long as there is a waiting population to receive her goods."

Family legend has it that he rode into town aboard the top of a freight car, was favorably impressed, and decided Pittsburg was his future home. How close is this to the truth? Probably not very; William had enough money for a rail ticket. After unearthing a family history written by my great-aunt Belle, I learned that he came to Pittsburg with more than a thousand dollars in his pocket, another loan from his father, which he used to open an exclusive shoe store, becoming one of the first merchants on Broadway Street.

Today, Broadway Street is a thoroughfare of modern commerce. But behind its facade of strip malls are the remnants of another century: foundations, sidewalks, cellars, and water wells in abandoned scrub fields; railroad equipment strewn across the ballasts of an old railroad bed; and the waste of old tipples and engine houses, traces of the town's industrial past.

Pittsburg was founded in 1876 as a depot point between Girard and Joplin. Capitalists from the Joplin area saw the depot location as essential to boosting profits in the greater Tri-State Mining District, a roughly twenty-five-hundred-square-mile area located in southeastern Kansas, southwestern Missouri, and northeastern Oklahoma. Little interest was taken in the town until the first coal shaft was sunk. Then, in 1877, a British-born entrepreneur named Robert Lanyon visited Pittsburg to survey prospects for an expanding zinc smelting business. Rich with coal, Pittsburg was the ideal location: Lanyon quickly purchased land and built a row of smelters at the edge of town, haloed in a crown of black smoke. "Smelters ran 24 hours a day, seven days a week," and the furnaces burned bright. It was a dirty, dangerous business, where miners might be crushed or severely scalded at any time. The voluminous amounts of burning coal used to smelt the ore also released sulfur and nitrogen oxides, which burned the eyes and lungs and caused acid rain, creating vast amounts of soot loaded with chemicals like lead and arsenic.

As the Kansas coal mines expanded over the next two decades, companies began to actively recruit miners. The first large influx of workers came from the Pennsylvania coalfields. Others came to Kansas from Oklahoma during labor disputes between 1882 and 1895, and in that same period, Black miners arrived from Alabama, replacing striking workers. Many of these workers stayed after the strike settled and, by 1900, made up 12 percent of the workforce. But until 1898, coal companies were in such dire need of miners, they sent agents further afield as well. In the ports of New York, agents met immigrants at the pier, offering free transportation to the Kansas coalfields—"paradise on Earth." Coal towns became "a polyglot area peopled by Italians, Germans, French, Belgians, and a variety of ethnic groups from the British Isles and the Austro-Hungarian Empire."

My maternal great-grandfather, James Kirkpatrick McCluskey, was one of those men. He arrived in Pittsburg from Scotland in 1887, although there's a chance he traveled by way of Pennsylvania, where his brother lived as a coal miner. He spent the rest of his life digging coal. His sons—all but my grandfather, the youngest of nine—followed him into the mines. The family first settled in Fleming, a mining camp about six miles southwest of town, and lived in at least three other camps before they finally were able to afford a move to Pittsburg, nearly two decades after James began working the mines.

My grandfather, William Ronald McCluskey, was born in Yale, a camp a few miles northeast of Pittsburg, close to the Missouri border. Early photographs show a desolate place with dirt roads and stubby trees. Camp houses—or, more appropriately, shacks—stood along rectangular lines of a survey, presenting a dull, uniform appearance. One reporter for a socialist newspaper described them in detail. "Coal soot has blackened the walls and ceilings" of the miners' homes, she wrote, "or ragged paper flutters from the walls. . . . Through the broken roof and frail sides the rains ruin the few possessions of the miner's family and drip down on his wretched bed."

These camps proved temporary. As coal diminished, mines were closed and dismantled, and new ones opened in the expanding coal fields. Miners frequently moved from mine to mine and camp to camp; houses, shacks, and other buildings were disassembled and moved on railroad flatcars or huge wagons pulled by mules. At each new site, the buildings were lined up in rows, dirt-surfaced roads and streets springing up between them. Immigrant families endured terrible living and working conditions. The number of mining injuries and deaths were common, overwhelming. Workers faced terrible conditions, including "cave-ins, falling rock, explosions, noxious gases, exposed shafts that were hundreds of feet deep, and unsafe levels of dust."

Workers were paid about two dollars per day, leaving families with little to subsist on. Many farmed and cared for livestock in their free time; others hunted and fished in streams near the mines, and some took up bootlegging to subsidize their family income. The consumption of whiskey in the camps was considerable. The state's prohibition laws meant liquor had to be distilled in secret, leading to increased criminality. The unruly reputation of the coalfields became so acute that Walter Stubbs, governor from 1909 to 1913, declared, "I might as well be governor of the Balkans." Over time, the coal camps would become known as the "Little Balkans," as I'd learned in my research on Edward. (It's a name that persists today: "Little Balkans Days," an annual Labor Day festival in Pittsburg, draws thousands to "pay homage to the region's history, ethnic diversity, and community spirit.")

The Little Balkans were also politically distinct. Crawford County developed into one of the most progressive regions in the state, known for its ardent and radical prolabor movement. The town of Girard, the county seat, became the intellectual center for the local socialist movement and the site of a national weekly, *Appeal to Reason*, which emerged as the most widely circulated socialist newspaper in the country. Eugene Debs, the socialists' famously perpetual candidate for president, made Girard his home for a time. Many other socialist leaders—including Mother Jones, a familiar figure to miners in the region—traveled to the area to speak at camp meetings and conventions.

"Socialist intellectuals seemed to understand the unique nature of Kansas mining and its accompanying radical politics as industrialized aberrations in the midst of an agrarian state," James N. Leiker has noted, "and therefore asserted an inclusive class identity—ameliorative of race, nationality, even gender—as a counter to rural conservatism."

Yet even as thousands of voters, motivated by frustration with industry, opted for socialist candidates in 1916, "the war made such successes short-lived. Extractive workers suffered many setbacks by 1920 in the form of declining prices, displacement by mechanization, and most significantly, lowered support for radical causes" as a postwar Red Scare began to spread through the country. The response to these changes was divided within organized labor, leading to internal conflict more generally, and to a number of protracted strikes in the Little Balkans specifically, under the leadership of socialist leader Alexander Howat.

Howat, the Scottish president of the United Mine Workers of America's District 14, was a charismatic, relentless fighter who had been nicknamed the "Bull of the Woods." His firsthand knowledge of coal mining—he began working in the mines at the age of ten—and the support of socialist intellectuals made him a folk hero in Kansas. He repeatedly challenged union leadership. When President Woodrow Wilson declared a 1919 nationwide coal strike illegal, the UMW called it off, but ten thousand Kansas miners, led by Howat, ignored the order. A few years later, in December 1921, thousands of wives, daughters, mothers, and sisters of coal miners striking under Howat marched in solidarity.

Christened the "Amazon Army" by the *Topeka Journal*, the women marched for days through Pittsburg and into camps, waving an American flag which they used to block the mines, symbolically drawing a line between patriot and traitor, between striker and worker. Some marchers beat workers, others threw pepper in their eyes, knocked over their lunch buckets, and doused them with coffee. Fights broke out in the camps, and after a few days, men joined in, bearing firearms. Fearing a popular uprising, the sheriff of Pittsburg stockpiled guns and rifles at a local hotel and requested help from Governor Henry Allen, who dispatched four Kansas National Guard troops—including a machine gun division—to take position in the camps. The troops were stationed in Pittsburg for several weeks. By early January, the National Guard began leaving and Howat called off the strike. The women of the march remained organized and turned their attention to politics, campaigning statewide for progressive candidates in the 1922 election. In the end, they successfully unseated several anti-strike incumbents and helped elect a labor-friendly Democratic governor, all of which changed the political atmosphere in the coal camp for several years.

My grandfather Edward was admitted to the bar that year, after graduating from the University of Kansas law school, and soon established the law firm of Patterson & Weir. He and Leah had married the year before, in Coffeyville, Kansas. Leah's father was proud of the union. Edward's mother, Ida, made the trip to the wedding on her own. The health of her husband, William, had broken in 1906, and he died in 1919, shortly after Edward returned from serving in World War I. My great-grandmother always said that *if, instead of going on the run, he had taken time out for himself, he might have lived longer.* I often wonder if Edward's professional and political ambitions weren't fueled by the loss of his father at this young age—or if he, like William, was simply helpless before the instinct to *go on the run.*

I have a studio portrait of the Patterson family that shows Edward as a little boy of nine or ten, close to the age my own father was when Edward died. In this early photograph, Edward's face is softer and rounder. He bears a striking resemblance to my father—and to me—when we were children. He's seated next to his parents, his sister, Belle, standing behind them. Edward looks a little bewildered, slightly unprepared. His gaze falls to the left, as does his father's: they may have watched the photographer leave the hood of the field camera before the shutter was forced open and then shut. The women, by contrast, stare straight into the lens. They wear white, high-collared Victorian dresses, Ida's with a brooch. Edward and his father are in suits with wide lapels. William wears a bow tie, slightly loose, slightly askew. His hair is cropped close and thin. He has a thick but perfectly trimmed mustache. The family is framed by a dark oval that the photographer has burned into the print, and most of William's body recedes into the shadows. Does he look frail? He looks like a small, slender man with puffy eyes. A sad pilgrim. A father who is beginning to disappear.

14.

It was the middle of March, two years after my father's death, but already spring in Kansas. A drought that had plagued the region in previous years was coming to a close: it had been raining for several weeks, which made the weather humid and unseasonably hot. Magnolias blooming, the air thick with sweetness. It wasn't the first time I had returned to Pittsburg since my trip with my mother to bury my father; at this point, I'd been back several times. On this visit, I spent the night with my cousin Krista, and the next morning, I got up early to take a drive.

On an impulse, I decided to drive by my grandmother Leah's house—not the house of my father's childhood, but the place where she lived for decades after Edward died. Driving there for the first time in many years, approaching from an unfamiliar direction, I made the wrong turn off Broadway. Afraid I might not recognize the house without a view of the porch, I drove slowly through the narrow streets until I reached an intersection I knew. There, a battalion of traffic barricades blocked the road. I parked the car, got out, and started walking.

Under a canopy of trees, I noticed a white clapboard house resting on a platform of cribbing and beams that hung over the edge of the sidewalk into the street, strange and out of place. It was a small structure, boxlike, a story and a half, but it looked enormous. From the street, I looked through the windows, hung with flowered curtains. The interior was dark. It was hard to know if the house was empty. I couldn't imagine why it was on the sidewalk. Relocation? Foundation repair? I slipped under the barricade tape and walked alongside the house to the curb. As I reached the sidewalk, I saw what was left of the house's concrete-slab basement crumbling into a gaping, cavernous sinkhole.

I called out into the yard.

—*Hello?*

No one answered.

The hole was frighteningly deep. From where I stood, it looked as if the lawn had been punched with a massive awl, exposing the ground's secret interior. A row of shrubs had been pulled into the void, littering the rim with branches and leaves, while broken concrete, pipe, and wire beetled everywhere. I had never seen anything like it. The terrifying, alien world of a sinkhole—the earth turning in on itself—an obvious metaphor. One I couldn't ignore.

That morning, staring at the hole, I felt as if I was looking into a realm that I could not enter. A world of dark earth, of broken rocks and minerals, of air and water, all the things that had always been there and would always be there—but which we don't very often consider, and the sight of which, for some reason, made my hands tremble. I looked down to see the fencing tremble, my fingers wrapped in its mesh.

I turned and looked across the street. There was my grandmother's house. The drone of traffic rose and fell in the distance. An oriole flashed in a nearby tree. A train ground to a halt. I looked up to the roof, where I could see a small strip of sky. I gazed in all directions: the streets were empty.

I walked toward the lawn I'd played in as a child. A high ceiling of clouds drifted above. My shadow stretched across the lawn and onto the sidewalk. I reached down to touch it, doubting its existence. As soon as my hands reached the grass, I sat down. I felt the familiar emptiness that had come with my father's death. I pressed my palms into the grass. The feeling didn't pass. It became entwined with what I saw, became a part of the grass, the drifting clouds, the cavernous hole.

A few days later, I found a map of Pittsburg from the Kansas Department of Health's Surface Mining Unit. The map, used as a reference for new construction projects and as a record of sinkhole emergencies, showed Pittsburg from above, a Google Earth photo of its streets and homes veined with thick red lines—an overlay of a 1944 geological map of the Pittsburg-Weir coal bed. The town once had a ready supply of coal within twenty to one hundred feet of the surface, but today, 80 percent of the area is undermined, pockmarked by abandoned prospects, cave-ins, and mine shafts, represented on the map. Sinkhole incidents marked with case numbers and yellow dots—a few of which also represented a confirmed underground room or tunnel, some as much as 150 feet deep—littered the image. I located my grandmother's house near the intersection of Olive and Euclid. An abandoned mine stretched from her front yard into the street, invisible below a row of cottonwood trees planted along the boulevard long ago.

—*Happens all the time around here*, Krista said when I told her about the sinkhole that afternoon. We were standing in the kitchen. She was buttering toast. *Do you want something to eat?*
    —*No thanks.*

She kicked off her shoes, and we both sat down at a counter separating the kitchen and the living room. When I explained the location of the hole I'd seen, Krista told me that the house where she first lived was just down the street and had collapsed into a sinkhole when she was three. I'd never learned any of this history.

    —*The house was humble and not worth saving. And the lot is still vacant. The potential of sinkholes has pursued me my entire life.*

Later, I learned that a sinkhole is essentially any hole in the ground created by erosion. It can be just a few feet across or large enough to swallow whole buildings. In Kansas, a sinkhole is sometimes called a snake hole, and they're well known; descriptions of sinkholes date back as early as the 1800s. The famous Meade salt sink flooded a wagon road in 1879. It was 60 feet deep and had a circumference of 610 feet. In 1927, a huge but shallow sink—200 feet long and 18 feet deep—developed in Mitchell County, attracting national attention. In 2005, federal agencies used a camera to search a 100-foot-deep sinkhole in Galena, Kansas, for two missing girls, after a man confessed to their murder.

Sinkholes occur naturally when rain, transformed into weak carbonic acid, eats away susceptible underground rock like limestone or gypsum. But there are also human-made sinkholes, caused by drilling, mining, construction, and broken water pipes. Sinkholes have plagued southeastern Kansas for years. On most occasions, these are small, like the hole that opened up in a farm field in Cherokee County, taking hold of the front end of a tractor. Other times, they're much worse. In 2006, a two-story apartment building in Galena was swallowed by a sinkhole that also destroyed the town's only remaining bar.

In the weeks that followed my sinkhole sighting, I would learn more. I looked at additional maps online and read geological abstracts and environmental reports published by the United States Bureau of Mines. I culled headlines from newspapers and watched terrifying videos of sinkholes swallowing cars, trucks, animals, people, and trees. I watched two people disappear in a subway tunnel; a dog fall away into a lawn; a row of cypress trees sink into a bayou; and a four-thousand-acre lake near Tallahassee drained instantly down a hole.

My preoccupation with sinkholes hasn't waned. I still follow them in the news, from the sensational to the banal. The *World Property Journal* declared 2013 the "Year of the Sinkhole" after several catastrophic events in Florida. One of these disasters was straight from a nightmare: a man named Jeff Bush screamed for help as a large sinkhole opened up under his bedroom and swallowed him alive. His body was never found. Word spread that year of Pennsylvania sinkholes in Allentown, Bethlehem, and North Londonderry Township. One of these holes ate a creek and drained a duck pond. In 2020, a sinkhole in the Westmoreland neighborhood of Gainesville, Florida, grew to more than one hundred feet wide, taking two houses and a swimming pool.

And then there's the forty-acre hole in Bayou Corne, Louisiana, where a salt mine owned by Occidental Petroleum and used as a storage reservoir for crude oil collapsed in 2012, releasing a stream of oil and natural gas that seeped into the aquifer and wafted into the community. I watched footage of the sinkhole belching out mini-earthquakes, videos of it sucking down trees. Most of the town's residents were evacuated and some never returned. Property buyouts by Texas Brine, the salt-mine operator of the cavern, followed. Today, the community has dwindled to a dozen or so families, many of whom remained in a protracted legal battle with both Texas Brine and Occidental Petroleum until a judge awarded them a large settlement in 2019. Disasters like this have done little to slow the expansion of injection mining. It's the price of doing business.

15.

Cherokee County, most of Crawford County, and a small part of Bourbon County—six hundred thousand acres in all—once belonged to the Wahzhazhe, or Osage, and served as a boundary between Missouri and what was then called Indian Territory. Fifty miles long and twenty-five miles wide, the area was known as the Neutral Lands. It was first forcibly ceded by the Wahzhazhe to the United States government in 1825 and then transferred to the Cherokee in 1835 as part of the Treaty of New Echota— the treaty that forced the exile of most remaining eastern tribes, including the Cherokee, via the brutal Trail of Tears. Most tribal members eventually settled present-day northeastern Oklahoma, but some ventured into the northern reaches of the Cherokee Nation, in what is now Kansas.

In 1842, in a state-sponsored effort to secure the land and the confinement of both the Wahzhazhe and the Cherokee, the military tried to install a base in the Neutral Lands, but then moved further north, to Bourbon County. Just a few years later, betraying established treaties, white people began settling in the area. The region's rich soil, ample water sources, and abundance of wild rye and other luxuriant grasses drew those settlers in high numbers.

They came without money. They came on foot, on horseback, and in covered wagons driven by oxen, mules, or horses; they came from Pennsylvania, Ohio, Illinois, and Iowa. They brought saws, hammers, axes, and nails; they brought revolvers; they laid their claims with a view to getting some of the area's timber. They plowed the earth and grew wheat, oats, and flax. They brought stoves, reapers, crushers, fanners; they brought leather, cornmeal, bacon, rice; they brought needles, pins, scissors; they harvested limestone and clay; they built houses and stores and schools and churches; they spread into the traditional homelands of the Wahzhazhe and more recent territory of the Cherokee people without authority of occupancy; they were squatters on the land.

Records suggest a growing white population on the Neutral Lands by the time of the Civil War. By the close of the war, and with the aid of the Homestead Act of 1862, many more white families (American-born and immigrant) had come to Crawford County, profiting from what scholar Keri Leigh Merritt calls "the most extensive, radical, redistributive governmental policy in US history." The population of Crawford County continued to increase steadily over the last decades of the century, paralleling the rise of coal mining in the 1870s through the 1890s.

At first glance, this contested, overworked region doesn't look like a landscape of ruins. But the symptoms of erosion rest just below the surface. The text of a catastrophic history is hidden beneath the earth, as if the land wants to be left alone with its grief. When I considered it, I felt recognition—the land, too, had something festering inside.

On my visits to Kansas, I took long drives in the country, walked down small creek beds and through the cemetery, visited tourist sites, ate at all the fried chicken joints (Pittsburg is the self-proclaimed fried chicken capital of Kansas), and spent hours in the public library and genealogical libraries searching for more information about the town and my family. *It's as if I am trying to remember myself,* I told one friend—*as if I am making a new place for myself.* Afterward, I would say Pittsburg was a kind of blank slate for me, a place where I could be unbounded but also oddly rooted; it was at once a diversion and a shrine. Throwing myself into the town's geography and history allowed me to temporarily look away from my father's death—or at least to look at it slantingly.

This became abundantly clear when I found myself driving to the small town of Weir one afternoon, looking for the spot where my paternal grandfather's body had been found. At that time, I had only newspaper accounts to refer to, and they had provided me with only the approximate location. But I believed that if I somehow found the right country road, I'd know by instinct the exact place. I drove into Weir and then headed west to what is now Liberty Road, a narrow dirt strip that cuts through corn and alfalfa fields. I drove up and down the road slowly, a world opening up in the small units of distance I traveled: the light over the fields, the heat in the air, the silence of the trees. A sudden feeling of sorrow gripped me. I pulled off the side of the road and got out of the car, momentarily shrouded in a cloud of dust. I left the car and walked further down the road toward a native tallgrass prairie. I walked straight into the field without thought. After a few hundred yards, I sat down. Beneath the bluestem grasses and side oats, I was surprised to find an abundance of growth: goldenrod, aster, and blazing star, all blooming under the cool shade of the tallgrasses. I took some soil into my hands and closed my eyes to take in its sweet fragrance, imagining things out of my reach. The particles, minerals, pores, gases; the red oxides of iron and clay; the biomantle of dead plants and animal tissue and all its living organisms; the mites, snails, beetles, springtails, worms, grubs.

When I opened my eyes, I felt my sadness temporarily lift. I felt my body and my mind loosen. After a while, I got up and went back to my car. A few years later, when I found the coroner's report for my grandfather's death, I would discover I had been fewer than five hundred yards from the place I was seeking.

———

Later, I walked a park trail in Pittsburg, following an old railroad bed through the west end of town. I passed Ninth Street, where my own immediate family history had begun. My mother had been a swim instructor at a public pool in the park. One hot afternoon, my father, too shy to approach her directly, wrote his name and number on a matchbook cover and left it near the lifeguard chair while she was on break. It's hard to know where I heard this story. I seem to remember my grandmother mentioning it once during a family dinner while everyone laughed, knowing my father had averted one of the cardinal rules of 1950s dating etiquette: men always did the asking. I walked the trail to the end and doubled back, immersed in childhood memories, evolving without chronology, barely comprehensible: I play in tall grass; I eat strawberries with sugar; I fill up on cheese sandwiches at lunch; I swing in an oak tree. One morning, I go down to the stream that runs at the bottom of the hill near my grandmother's house; on another, in the shade of the trees, the stream smells cold and goes dark.

And then a thought, clearer than others: I had a genetic trace here, this place was a part of me—a place I could possess and one that possessed me.

16.

Above my desk I keep a picture postcard of a Pittsburg strip pit. I found and bought it on eBay in the midst of my obsessive research; it came wrapped in brown paper from someone in Illinois, accompanied by a handwritten note that said, "Enjoy!" The photograph shows six men standing in the pit, dwarfed by the landscape that surrounds them: the clouds hovering above, a horizon of green trees, and a sheer face of rock behind them. An additional man rests on a hill at the edge of the pit, looking like a spectator, legs relaxed but spread wide. Two tiny children stand on either side of him. We can't see any of the men's faces. They aren't the true subject of this image. We see—or the photograph insists I see—the cavern of rock and stubbled ground where they stand and which they must feel beneath their feet.

The photograph is undated, but I'd guess it was taken in the early 1900s. In some open fields, the ground was once so riddled with holes that it resembled a moonscape. Eventually these sites grew into large commercial operations. In Treece, Baxter Springs, and even Weir, there are still devastated stretches of land: spoil banks, broken rock, and mine pits. Spoil banks resemble the layered rock formations you might find in a desert but are made entirely of waste—tailings from lead and zinc mining.

Between them, channels fill with water, made orange by acid-rock drainage. In the early 1980s, the Bureau of Mines cataloged the physical dangers still present in the Tri-State Mining District using state geological surveys and discovered "more than 1,500 open shafts" and nearly five hundred sinks in the area, "including 599 mine hazards in and around Galena" (a section of which was known as "Hell's Half-Acre"). In 1994 and 1995, through a collaborative effort between local citizens and the Environmental Protection Agency (EPA), the mine shafts and collapses in Galena were filled and covered in topsoil. But sinkholes still occur.

Near Pittsburg, strip mining left the land marked with deep ditches. But early in in the town's history, an effort was made to remediate these places. In 1928, Spencer Chemical planted the ridges of abandoned pits with alfalfa and catalpa trees. Although the surface soil was contaminated and held vast amounts of shale, the vegetation thrived. And so, fueled by the experiment's success, residents informally reforested many of the other stripped lands nearby with native trees like elm, cottonwood, willow, and wild cherry. That same year, Pittsburg citizens bought and donated four hundred acres composed mostly of strip pits to Kansas. This area was developed by the Civilian Conservation Corps and became Crawford State Park, a forested destination whose old pits have become deep and narrow lakes. Some of them filled naturally, while others were flooded and stocked with bass, bluegill, and channel catfish. The idea caught on and soon other pits in abandoned mining camps surrounding Pittsburg were crowded with fish.

My mother's father liked to go angling in these lakes on weekends. He ended his life by drowning in one of those pits, the site of a favorite fishing hole.

———

I was in my twenties before I learned that my grandfather William McCluskey died by suicide. Years before, someone—maybe my grandmother, Alta Faye—had told me he died of heart failure, but it didn't come up again.

My mother and I were walking through the Minneapolis Institute of Art when she said, rather off-handedly, *I think I finally understand his death.*

—*What do you mean?* I asked.

—*I mean that I can finally accept the way he died.*

—*A heart attack?*

—*Who told you that?* she said.

—*I don't know. You?*

—*No*, she said. *Not me.*

We were standing in a gallery among Georgia O'Keeffe's works. I don't remember how my grandfather's death had slipped into the conversation. Even if my mother believed I already knew the story, she might have chosen this moment to revisit it because she couldn't bear a prolonged conversation on the matter. Or maybe the emotional proportion of the paintings—the oversized petals and delicate contours of the flower's shape, the resplendent skulls and black crosses—spurred her memory and provoked her to speak: a mnemonic reckoning, more than story.

—He took his own life on your birthday.

A long silence followed. Images flooded my mind: stacked white plates rimmed with frosting surrounding a half-eaten cake, a garbage bag bulging with crushed party hats and ribbons slumped at my mother's feet. I remember her cries were guttural, heavy sobs erupting from nothingness, her arms submerged in water at the kitchen sink. How many times had my mother cried like that on my birthday? Enough that, as a child, I came to believe that my mother's sadness was connected to me. Whatever I felt in that moment at the museum—sympathy, terror, relief, something else I doubt I could name—gave way to a thought that my life had been deeply shaped by a remote and unknown past. My mother's pain somehow suddenly made sense.

She was the first to break the silence hanging in the air between us.

—Ready to go? she asked.

For a moment, I could only stand there. She turned and began walking toward the gallery exit. I followed.

We said nothing on the drive home. I could think of nothing to say. In the following days, weeks, months, then years, I'd also held back, keeping with my family's reticence. It wasn't until my father died that my mother and I spoke of these events again.

My quest for information had become a private task of mourning—and with time, my mother's father also became part of the story. My desire to know him progressed out of my search for Edward, which had in turn evolved out of a need to understand my own father. What unified the three of them in my imagination was not just suicide, however obvious and important that link might be, but the sensation that they represented *fathers*. Who were these men, these fathers? They were hard to see clearly. Their lives had, for the most part, gone the way of secrecy. They had left so little behind to their children, except to make us angry, disappointed, coolly detached. My parents had done exactly what their fathers wanted— consigned them to shadows—but I was going to drag them into the light, as best I could.

———

My mother's father was sixty-two when he died. He'd been a father for almost forty years. His body was retrieved from the lake on my fourth birthday: September 26, 1967.

I have no real memory of him. My mother describes him as a kind, guiding force, but for both of us, he persisted in the pleasure of materials: food, smoke, wood, and clay. He was referenced in passing ways, a ghost conjured by the solidity of things. *Pa's favorite, Daddy would like this, Pa would not approve*; by the pleasure of a good meal, a weightless slice of cheese, the sealed body of a pie cooling in a window, the air tinged with the scent of ripe fruit.

My mother has always maintained that my grandfather and I shared a unique bond. I was a serious child,
she says. I rarely smiled. I stared at adults with an unsettling intensity, which often made her uncomfortable.
But when I first met my grandfather, she tells me, I burst
into a fit of laughter. I don't remember any of this. When
I look at photographs from the visit she describes, I don't
see happiness. I see an infant's look of bewilderment.

After his death, my mother claimed that William
watched over and protected me. Once, when I was
twelve, I accompanied her to a psychic reading at a new
age bookstore in a then-gritty part of Minneapolis. It
was a hot, damp August afternoon, possibly my grandfather's birthday. I was just tagging along, but the psychic

(or *intuitive*, as she referred to herself) suggested as soon as she caught sight of us that a portion of the reading include me. My mother hastily agreed. We were led to a curtained loft above the bookstore and seated around a small, empty table. The intuitive closed her eyes and leaned back in her chair.

—*I am sensing a strong presence*, she said. She opened her eyes and looked at me. *Someone protecting you. A man. Have you ever had the sensation that someone was touching your head? He says he makes himself known by touching your hair.* She paused. *Wait, there is a name. William.*

Out of the corner of my eye, I saw my mother flinch. Tears began to glaze her eyes.

I was soon after excused, left to wander through books a floor below. In the car on the way home, I watched my mother's hands tense on the wheel.

———

Born in Yale, my grandfather lived in the Pittsburg area most of his life. Founded by the Western Coal and Mining Company in the late 1800s, Yale had grown, by the time my grandfather was born, into a town with a post office, stores, churches, schools, and a Missouri Pacific Railroad Company station. Still, it was a world away from Pittsburg. According to varying historical accounts, Yale consisted of anywhere from one hundred to five hundred workers. The population surged after two union strikes in the 1800s, when company agents lured nonunion Black miners from Jefferson

County, Alabama. The coal companies took advantage not just of the workers' skill but of their desire to immigrate out of the Jim Crow South, by hiring "members of the black community . . . to extoll the virtues of Kansas; availability of good jobs, higher wages, more privileges and few restrictions." This picture of the state was overblown.

Throughout the summer of 1899, trains departed Birmingham for Kansas, carrying about thirteen hundred workers in total, along with their families. They hadn't been told they'd be breaking a strike, but as the trains went west, there were signs the miners were at risk. Guards stepped aboard the trains in Tennessee, and as they crossed into Kansas, passengers were told to avoid windows. When the train finally pulled into Fleming, they were hustled into stockades flanked by US Marshals in six different camps—including Yale and Nelson, where my great-grandparents lived at the time—to protect the Alabamans from the strikers.

Was my great-grandfather a union man, one of these strikers? No one knows for sure, but it's unlikely. First, he had seven children by then (my grandfather was yet to be born). With so many mouths to feed, he may have had no choice but to work. Miners who participated in strikes risked not being rehired. Second, when the strike happened, the family was new to camp, and they ultimately lived in Nelson for five years. The strike ended in September of 1899, with little violence. The stockades were dismantled and the Alabamans were encouraged to stay, a strategy company owners used to keep the mines up and running should there be a future strike. The new miners were moved into houses with floors made from the stockade's lumber that the company rented for seven dollars a month.

It's unclear how long the camp survived. My grandfather's family moved to Yale in 1905, around the time the coal seam in Nelson was depleted. I searched for photographs of the stockades, of the camps in this period, but came up empty-handed. I found only a few photographs of Nelson at all. One image, bleaker than others I had seen, felt like a rebuttal of my Pittsburg postcard, with its turned earth and seven men: a hazy snapshot of the mine tipple, with no people in the frame, just two smokestacks towering against the horizon.

———

At nineteen, my grandfather met Alta Faye Norvell from Neosho, Missouri. The moment he set eyes on her, he was bewitched. She was perhaps the most beautiful woman he'd ever seen. In March 1925, they married in Miami, Oklahoma, after eloping there with another couple. Albertina, my grandmother's closest friend, and her soon-to-be husband were marrying without family consent. My grandparents had agreed to serve as witnesses, while getting married themselves.

Back then, at least according to family lore, Oklahoma was a quick and legal destination for out-of-state elopements. The trip from Pittsburg could easily be made in a day. My grandparents and their friends drove down Quincy Street, out of town, then south on Route

69 straight past Cherokee, Weir, and the valleys of Baxter Springs. Once they crossed the border into Oklahoma, they saw strings of derricks and mills, coal trucks and hulking draglines in the fields.

They stood in their overcoats before the county judge. My grandmother didn't wear white. The wedding, after all, had been hastily planned: the civil ceremony brief, their vows secular. It's hard to imagine what they might have done afterward. Miami wasn't the town it would later become. Back then, Route 66 hadn't yet been established and the glorious Coleman Theatre didn't exist. There was more to do in Pittsburg. They probably got back in the car and drove home. The women sat together in the back of an early American automobile—their friendship cemented for a lifetime.

Years later, Albertina's marriage dissolved, and she became an early and unexpected link between the two sides of my family. The same woman who rode in the car with my grandmother, Alta Faye's best friend, would eventually become Edward Patterson's secretary—and then his mistress.

—

It was my mother who told me about the connection. In his notes about Edward's suicide, my father had written, *Mother was going to leave. Mother knew of the other woman. Albertina—was his secretary.*

I emailed my mother. *Do you know anything about Edward's secretary?* I wrote. *Maybe you know her last name?*

I wasn't prepared for her answer, which was both fluent and expressive. *This is the development which led to the total breakdown of the Patterson family,* she wrote back. *It was well into my life history (I wish that I had kept a diary) that my mother confided to me that she and my father had eloped.*

—*The ironic piece of the story,* she continued, *is Albertina became, somehow, Edward Patterson's legal secretary, for his law practice in Frontenac, Kansas, and when he was elected to Congress, went to Washington, DC, with him. I remember being totally astounded that my family had in any, any way been involved with the Patterson family. I did not know this when I met your father, and later married him. I do not know if he, in fact, ever knew either, but I would guess not, since we never talked about it.*

As for my mother's parents, after their elopement: they went back to living with their families, keeping their marriage secret. My grandfather's parents had just returned to Pittsburg after a decade of living in a camp near Arma or Mulberry. His siblings had all left Pittsburg and would never return. James moved to Oregon, Walter to California, and Jenny to Osage, Kansas; John traveled to Utah to work in the Castle Gate Mine and died in a 1924 explosion, one of the worst mining disasters in the country. Their exodus might be explained by any number of factors. Coal was one of America's ailing industries in the 1920s, and it was a turbulent era in Pittsburg's labor history.

My mother always says her father survived by creativity and wit. In her telling, his bounding imagination and embrace of risk carried him out of poverty. Luck was also on his side. He was too young to be deployed in World War I, and as coal production declined, the pressure for him to enter the Pittsburg mines dissolved. In 1924, he enrolled in Pittsburg Business College. Afterward, he found a job at Pittsburg Pottery, on the north side of town. The pottery opened in 1888, near one of many smelters in north Pittsburg owned by the Lanyon family. The Lanyons allowed a pottery kiln to be set up on the site, taking advantage of the excess heat, to produce stoneware. By 1913, A. K. and E. V. Lanyon had broken the pottery company into an independent business, and by my grandfather's time, the plant was owned by a group of local businessmen. William started as the company's stenographer, but was quickly made a manager. By 1930, he was superintendent. He and Alta Faye bought their first house. Their budget was meager, but they deployed it with taste. My grandparents were headed for a life far richer and happier than their parents could have imagined.

While Pittsburg Pottery was a commercial enterprise—a factory, more than anything—my grandfather's love of ceramics and clay pushed him and his partners to channel their energy in innovative ways, helping to separate the work from that of other local clay industries. The company began producing flowerpots, submitting them to trade with great success and expanding production to include stoneware jars, mixing bowls, and rabbit feeders; my grandfather molded small planters out of my mother's baby shoes.

But there were difficulties too. In the late 1930s, my mother says, the plant's employees organized a strike for higher wages. She recalls that my grandfather had a stake in the company at this point and was part owner of the business, although some of the (spotty) historical records suggest otherwise.

They threw stones at his car, she told me. *He sat at the kitchen table and cried. He was devastated. He couldn't see a way to make it work, so he just gave up. I don't think he ever got over it.* He left the company at the end of summer 1939.

At its peak, the pottery took orders in twenty-three states, displaying its wares in custom-built yellow trucks driven by four sales representatives across the country. There was enough high-grade stoneware clay in Pittsburg to last forever, but the plant closed down in the 1990s, a consequence of economic globalization. During one of my visits, I drove out to see the site. The old wooden beams of the building had caved in and were overtaken by vegetation, but the remains of a few beehive kilns were still standing inside, vented from the bottom to an enormous, intact smokestack. Bricks and pottery shards were strewn around the floor and at the base of each kiln. One entire wall had collapsed and was marred by smoke. A few years later, the site was fully demolished and the smokestack brought down.

When my grandfather left the pottery, his prospects may have been grim. Physical labor was easy enough to find in Pittsburg, but higher-paying jobs were more difficult to come by, and by then William was thirty-seven years old, with two children to support. His upwardly mobile life might have easily taken a bad turn. The war saved him: construction on a new weapons-grade ammonia nitrate plant was just beginning in nearby Galena. He started as a midlevel manager working the swing shift. Prosperity, in the form of a secure salary, had found him again.

After the war, the government sanctioned the use of

ammonia nitrate as fertilizer to make use of the many ordnance facilities that had sprung up over the years. The plant began operating under the name of Spencer Chemical; in 1964, it was purchased by Gulf Oil. At his retirement four years later, my grandfather was vested a large share of stock, which paid off handsomely. The company's profits had soared in the previous decade, as Gulf rapidly diversified and became active across the whole spectrum of the oil industry—exploration, production, transport, and refining. Expansion was so successful that Gulf's growth rate during the 1950s was twice that of the United States economy. My grandfather had struck it rich.

17.

William's suicide came six months after he retired. In a studio portrait taken near the end of his life, he stares straight into the camera as if about to speak, a tender half smile on his lips. His eyes carry a hint of melancholy, a wistful acceptance, as if he knows that life will soon be swept away. A small reflection flashes on the edge of his horn-rimmed glasses, and when I look closely, I notice the sheen of his forehead, the dark shine of his hair, and the faint but distinct impression left by a hatband over his right ear.

My grandfather's hat was virtually as necessary as his glasses. He wore it while he worked in the yard and often indoors as well. The day he died, he left his hat on the kitchen table, alerting my grandmother that something was terribly wrong. According to my cousin Krista—who herself learned this from our grandparents' housekeeper—he also left a note, which Alta Faye read and promptly destroyed.

At our house in St. Paul, the news of his death came via an unexpected call the morning of my birthday. Alta Faye phoned only after the body had been found, after the agonizing hours of searching the day before, after the unfolding tragedy of the morning. The news, when delivered, was not only a shock but also a painful reminder of the punishing separation that had developed between my mother and her parents, a consequence of her leaving Kansas for good. Her sister, Rosemary, was still in Pittsburg. When my grandfather went missing, Rosemary kept Alta Faye company all through the night. She was still at my grandparents' house when the Crawford County sheriff, a family friend, came to announce the search was over.

William had last been seen alive the previous afternoon, a Monday. He left home to fill the car with gas. He never returned. Two hundred and fifty people came out to search for him that night, despite rain. Searchers found his car at the edge of a flooded strip pit just outside the small town of Cherokee. Firemen used a grappling hook to dredge the bottom of the lake. After the water settled, divers from the Pittsburg Fire Department located the body. The immediate cause of death was *(a) drowning (b) both wrists entered fatally* (c) *both calves of legs lacerated.* A compact, slim pocketknife was found at the site. The rearview mirror of the car was smashed.

My mother arrived in Kansas a few hours after receiving the news. The plant where my grandfather had worked sent a private company jet for her. She speaks of this now as a small miracle, a novelty in that period of history when flight was not yet a common luxury. My father and I followed a day later, making the ten-hour car drive without rest, dogs in tow. But not before he managed to proceed with my birthday party, scheduled for that afternoon. I don't remember any of these events: the call, the party, the drive.

When William died, my grandparents had been living in a one-story brick rambler on the outer edge of town, in a neighborhood with no sidewalks and wide streets. The front yard was an open expanse of lawn, neatly manicured, with little adornment. Alta Faye's taste was understated if not puritan, and this patch of lawn, seeded and fertilized to a perfect density, was austere. Her backyard, however, was wild and unkempt. A catalpa tree towered over the house, vines and lichen sprawling up its trunk, and wild roses rambled up the high fence erected for the sake of her toy poodle, Toby, who liked to run outdoors. (More to the truth, the yard served as a holding pen for the dog when he misbehaved, which was often.)

Alta Faye spent the rest of her life in this house. On our visits, we spent nearly all our time in the den, a room that smelled of perfumed soap and was covered in honey-colored wood and filled with furniture, books, and magazines. A large television occupied one corner and was always left on. Unless there was occasion for a more formal gathering, when we ate it was in the den, on TV trays mounted on small metal stands. In the evening, after long day of visiting, I would stretch out across large corduroy cushions on the floor or sit to read a book on the leather couch, my feet sprawled over its arm, a posture I was solely afforded there, in the den. In other rooms of the house, I was commonly scolded. *Don't bother the dog. Listen before you speak. Take off your shoes. Sit yourself straight. Don't touch anything.* Alta Faye herself spent days in the den, and I knew not to interrupt her there: privately smoking, gazing out the window, wearing a silk nightgown or a bathrobe. She rarely dressed, especially as she aged, and only then to leave the house; she was buried, at her request, in a rose-colored nightgown trimmed in lace.

The front rooms carried the must of a museum. The living room was immaculately clean, as if inhabited only in the most utilitarian of ways. The walls were bone white, the furniture—a sitting chair, couch, and coffee table—stuffed into corners, leaving open a cold and unwelcoming expanse of carpeting. Near the door, an upright piano and its bench rested under an ornate, gold-framed mirror. I don't believe anyone ever played the piano, though there are many photographs of me as a child sitting before it, an apparent ritual of our visits. In one overexposed photograph, washed in pink, my father, mother, and I are squeezed onto the bench. My torso slumps between their hips, my feet don't yet reach the floor. I am looking at the camera with a slightly bored expression, a thin smile. In another, I am years older, seated with Krista, who wears a new dress and Easter hat. Above her, on top of the piano, bursts a vase of daisies, and among the curve of their petals is a trace of my grandmother's head, ringed by the bulb's flash.

On those visits to Pittsburg, my grandmother often insisted we visit the cemetery. She didn't drive, so we usually made the trip in our own car. We typically didn't leave the car. Weather was the excuse. *Too hot*, my grandmother would say with her hand thrust out an open window, which meant we'd spend a few minutes idling near the gravesite, visible from the road, glancing at William's headstone from our seats.

I felt no particular love for this ritual.

My grandmother lived well beyond my grandfather. When she died, I helped my parents pack up her house. I'd just turned thirty-one. It had been years since I learned that William had died by suicide, but in the rooms of Alta Faye's house, there were still pictures of him everywhere: a stark contrast to how my mother would respond to and absorb the suicide of her own husband. The black-and-white portrait of William taken late in his life still hung in the bedroom next to a similar photograph of Alta Faye. When I took the pictures off the wall, a square of brightly hued paint appeared, the rest of the wall faded in the twenty-seven years since his death.

That morning, my father and I took my parents' two dogs for a walk. He stepped out of the house first and I followed. As my father was often quiet on these visits to Kansas, I knew it was best not to talk. We turned onto a street—one I didn't know or remember—dense with a canopy of elms. Through all the years my parents and I had been visiting Pittsburg, much of the town remained unknown to me. Occasionally, my mother would point out a structure through the window of the car and say something vague like, *There's the old house*, but we never stopped to visit or appreciate these places. My father never made these references, and, in fact, would drive on only a few streets—Broadway, Quincy, Rose—so that even as an adult, my main point of reference was my grandmother's rambler.

Now, as we walked, the street widened, divided by an elaborately landscaped median, into an older and wealthier part of town. The houses were large and stately, with expansive open porches and brick sidewalks. After a few blocks, my father turned down an alley. Again, I followed without comment. He stopped abruptly a couple of yards ahead, pulling the dogs back, distracted by something in a nearby yard. I stopped too, peering through bushes into the lawn, thinking my father had sighted an animal. I didn't see anything. My father stood motionless, still staring off. After a long period of silence, he said:

—*There used to be a cherry tree in the yard.* After another pause, he gestured toward the back of the house. *And that was my bedroom window.*

I looked up at the small window, veiled by a sheer white curtain. A wind pushed the hem, and I watched it waving in the darkened space. My father's childhood home suddenly, unexpectedly, existed. Red brick with ivory and black trim and wrapped with an open porch, the house had tall and generous windows, some dressed with deep blue curtains. In the yard flourished petunias, gladiolas, and marigolds. My father and I stood in the alley for several minutes. The stillness between us was amplified by the smallest movement: a bee hovering in the air, a shadow falling from the brim of my father's baseball hat across his face, his jaw throbbing as he clenched his teeth. We stood for a few more moments, and then he began to walk. When we reached the end of the alley, I turned once more to see the house, nearly out of view: the house where he lived as a boy; the house with his books and toys; the house where his sister and mother and father slept.

Back at my grandmother's house, I found my grandfather's gold-plated Bulova watch in a nightstand. Rectangular and small by today's standards but inescapably elegant, with a gold-and-silver expandable band, silver satin dial, and raised gilt European numerals. I started wearing it the day of Alta Faye's funeral: November 20, 1994.

By January, the watch had stopped working. I wasn't surprised. How could it still be running, after all? But when the hands stilled, I felt adrift, so I took the watch in to a repair shop. Behind the counter, the shop owner stood, a magnifying glass strapped to his forehead.

—*You've taken great care of this watch*, he said as he gently pried open the back casing. *This all looks like original hardware.*

—*I don't know*, I said. *I inherited it from my grandfather.*

—*Well, he made a point of keeping it clean. Take a look.*

He set the watch down on a glass counter. I saw a maze of wheels and gears. With a small pair of pointed tweezers, he pointed to the watch's outer wheel.

—*See these hash marks?* he asked. Along the wheel's edge was a string of short lines, carefully etched into the plated surface. *A watchmaker will mark a watch like this every time it's cleaned. It looks like this watch has been serviced every year for at least twenty-five years.*

I watched him drop his tweezers and pick up another tool to begin loosening the tiny screws on the watch plate. The very precise image of Alta Faye that I had preserved, of her silently smoking in the den, splintered in my mind. It was hard to reconcile the strict, taciturn woman I knew with the person who had dutifully preserved the memory of my grandfather in the ritualized care of his watch. In that moment, I was overcome with the realization that maybe all along, I'd misjudged her, mistaken her grief for indifference. How could it be otherwise? I considered the calendar. On what annual occasion had she serviced the watch? Birthday? Holiday? Wedding anniversary? Or the other anniversary, of his death?

—*This should be an easy fix*, the watchmaker said, handing me a receipt. *Should be ready early next week.*

I took the slip of paper and left the store, stepping out into the falling snow.

18.

September 25, 1967. Monday. The sun not yet on the horizon, windows black against the light in the den, where I imagine my grandfather William sits. Unable to sleep, he's methodically cleaning a collection of tobacco pipes. There are six in all. He's laid them out in a row on a tray next to a table-sized circular rack where they're normally stored, polished to a cherry sheen. The pipes vary in size, shape, and ornateness, the most decorative with a hand-painted porcelain bowl cast in the form of a bear's head, the animal's snout jutting out in the front, rounded ears on the pipe's black stem. The pipe is difficult to clean and to hold. William thinks of it as an object of beauty, not function; his attention therefore frequently lands elsewhere when it comes to a smoke, as evidenced by the scars his teeth have made in pipes like the one he is now cradling in his hand. Using a knife, he begins cutting the caked tobacco back in the bowl, shaving a hole large enough for the pipe reamer, which he uses to trim the cake to the thickness of a dime. He twists the reamer slowly, carefully. The blade leaves a trail of carbon dust in its wake. Periodically, my grandfather stops to empty the tobacco chamber, tapping the pipe lightly on a hankie spread out on the tray. Now he rims the pipe's bowl with his finger and ash smears on his skin. He touches the mound of crushed tobacco, sifting flakes between his fingers, before he shakes the hankie into a wastebasket on the floor. When he's finished, he arranges the pipes in the rack and sets it up on a shelf in the den. He stands to admire them briefly, then leaves the room to wash his hands.

In the hall, he notices the clock mounted above a hallway table. Eight in the morning. When he reaches the bathroom, he gently shuts the door behind him. He waits, as if to muster some energy, before he turns on the light, which flickers to brightness above the mirror. He removes his glasses and sets them next to the sink. He scrubs his hands first, filling the basin with soap and water, then rinses his face. When the house falls quiet, he can hear a distant train whistle, the sound of a car passing on a nearby street.

He enters the bedroom quietly. My grandmother turns in her sleep. He reaches for the closet door and picks out a suit and a pair of polished shoes. He finds a cleanly pressed shirt, socks, and underwear in a nearby drawer, arranging the entire outfit on the end of his bed. Silently, he gets dressed. Soon my grandmother is fully awake, her arm stretching out from under the sheets to reach the alarm clock on the bedside table.

—*Sorry to wake you*, he says.

—*You haven't*, she says. *It's about time I get up anyway. Ernestine will be here soon. She's starting in the den today—so stay out.*

—*What time?* he asks.

—*What?*

—*What time will she be here?*

Alta Faye reaches for her glasses and frowns at the clock.

—*Half an hour*, she says.

—*I'll finish up, then.*

—*What's that?*

—*Cleaning pipes*, he mutters as he leaves the room to retrieve the morning newspaper from the front stoop.

Back in the den, my grandfather sits in an easy chair in the corner, out of view of the open door. He can hear Alta Faye in the kitchen, the clinking of a spoon against her coffee cup and the sound of the housekeeper's key turning in the door.

He joins my grandmother in the kitchen, dropping the newspaper on the table. She makes him some toast and pours him a glass of orange juice. He never drinks coffee. She never allows herself juice. He smears his toast with jam. She forks sliced fruit. They eat in silence, a daily ritual.

Later, he cleans and straightens the garage and then mows the lawn, using an old push mower bought years ago. He remembers the pristine and shiny glint of the machine's blades when it was new. He remembers how easily it used to cut. Now long grass bends under the reel and he has to make several passes. It takes longer than he expected, and the work is tedious.

After cutting the grass, he edges the lawn near the sidewalk and driveway and trims the shrubs in front of the house, using a pair of long hedging shears. As he works, his mind drifts down the block, down Quincy Street, down a country road, out to the edge of Second Cow Creek, near the spoil banks where he fished as a boy. He remembers the earthy smell of the muddy banks and the sheen of water, the sun on his back, the apples he sometimes found in his lunch pail, slices of his mother's honey-baked ham and buttered biscuits.

By the time he's collected the trimmings and branches and bundled them into stacks, it's almost noon. He dusts himself off and goes back into the house. His mouth is dry, a side effect of the medication he's been prescribed. After lunch, he takes a nap in his easy chair, another symptom of his antidepressant; he's drowsy in the afternoon, burdened with insomnia at night.

Later, my grandfather emerges from sleep with a gasping breath and is instantly awake, jolted by the sound of the television. It's just after one in the afternoon. Alta Faye has left the house on a shopping trip. My grandfather kicks down his chair into a sitting position and shakes the legs of his trousers. He stretches and slowly rises out of the chair.

In the kitchen, he retrieves the car keys from a hook on the wall. *I'm going downtown to fill up the car,* he says to the housekeeper, and then exits through the back door into the garage. As he pulls out of the driveway, he realizes he's forgotten his hat, which he left on the table. But it's too late. He can't go back.

He drives west on Quincy Street. After crossing the junction with Route 69, he veers left, toward his favorite fishing hole, down a gravel road, and into a small thicket of woods. It's late afternoon, the day sweltering. He stops the car near the edge of the water, atop a flat ridge. He stares at the water's surface and tries to relax. The idea of drowning paralyzes him; he fears the body's inclination to fight.

But how else?

He smashes the rearview mirror with his fist. Shards fall on the seat and floor of the car. He collects a few larger pieces, rolls up his sleeve, and runs the edge of one along his wrist. It's not sharp enough to cut. He tries another. It makes a shallow mark that doesn't bleed. He rifles through the glove compartment of the car, tossing maps, insurance documents, and a mileage log aside. At the back, he finds a silver pocketknife, small enough to conceal in his hand. He holds it above the steering wheel, examining it for a moment, before raising one pant leg and then the other. The knife cuts sharply, deeply, rends through the calf muscle until blood begins to darken the gray wool of his suit. My grandfather's legs needle acutely as he steps out of the car. He cuts each arm, carefully tracing the radial artery—first the left and then the right. Finally, he staggers to the water and walks into the lake.

19.

According to Krista, sixteen at the time of his death, my grandfather had been diagnosed with atherosclerosis nearly a year before he died. When she told me this, it was late winter, two years after my father's suicide. We were sitting on the couch in her living room. I had been looking through a collection of my grandmother's photo albums that my cousin had saved.

Krista has spent most of her life in Pittsburg. She's twelve years older than me. Growing up, we didn't spend a lot of time together, but as a child I always liked and admired her. She's smart and funny and exceedingly practical. She lives in a house that was once a Pentecostal church, replete, she jokes, with snake handlers. The living room, where the congregation likely gathered, is cavernous. For a number of years, she worked as a journalist for the *Morning Sun*, the town's daily newspaper, but after tiring of a reporter's rigorous and unpredictable schedule, she took an administrative job at the former Mt. Carmel Regional Medical Center, just outside of town. There she established the Community Health Center of Southeast Kansas, originally an outreach service of the hospital. The program grew; my cousin cut ties with the hospital and assumed leadership of the nonprofit organization, establishing fifteen more low-cost health care clinics in the region. Everyone recognized her work, and she knew everyone in town.

Krista resembles her father more than her mother, Rosemary, so we don't exactly look like family. On my mother's side, not only was she the only person left in town but she had also fully taken up the task of archiving and preserving our family history. For as long as I could remember, she had collected photographs and memorabilia, carefully documenting their origins.

Surgery, Krista said, was recommended to address my grandfather's condition, though—like my father—he seems not to have pursued that course of action. Troubled by the prognosis, he plunged into a depression ("Mr. McCluskey was said to have been despondent lately," one newspaper article about his death noted). Krista doesn't remember his illness herself. She heard about it from my aunt Rosemary, who also told her that, a few months before his death, William was prescribed an antidepressant. There's no way of knowing his exact prescription, but it was most likely a monoamine oxidase inhibitor, an early and popular class of antidepressants that carried some side effects, including, on rare occasions, anxiety, agitation, restlessness, and increased risk of suicidal thoughts. Krista assumes the medication triggered William.

—*I've never heard him described as depressed*, I said.

—*The benevolent parent*, she replied.

She got up and left the room, then returned few moments later, carrying a small tin box.

—*I found this in the garage. It's from Mother's house. I thought you'd like to see it.*

In the wake of her mother's recent death, Krista had begun the slow and agonizing process of sorting through possessions, all of which, for the moment, were housed in her garage. Even though we were in different stages of mourning, we had the shared experience of loss and, for a time, I felt closer to her than anyone else in the family. That was part of what kept me coming back to Pittsburg.

—*I've never seen it before,* she said. *It seems strange to find it now, especially right before your visit.*

It was roughly the size of a small tackle box, made of aluminum and painted a dull green. The hinges, stiff and rusty, squealed as I pushed open the lid. Small bits of enamel pooled and chipped at the corners. The box had belonged to my grandmother; her name was written in perfect script on a paper address label glued to the lid. Inside, a newspaper clipping with details of my grandfather's death appeared atop a folded white handkerchief. I took everything out and spread the contents in my lap. In addition to the clipping, there was a copy of my grandfather's death certificate, his diploma from Pittsburg Business College, a bill of sale for a new car, a photograph of my grandparents, and a pocketknife.

I couldn't help but think of the box my mother had saved immediately following my father's death, and its odd but poignant contents: keys, a money clip, his driver's license, his wedding ring. I read the death certificate first—I couldn't help myself—and there were the words describing his suicide. It was here I first learned of the exact circumstances.

—*Did you read this?*

—*No*, Krista said.

—*He cut himself first. Jesus.*

She took the small document, no bigger than a large index card, from my hand, and looked at it briefly.

—*He was nothing if not thorough*, she said matter-of-factly.

I studied the photograph of my grandparents. In it, they are middle-aged, walking down the middle of an empty street, dressed to the hilt. My grandmother wears an ankle-length fur coat and my grandfather has on a three-piece suit, a top hat, and spats. They look like movie stars. For a moment, I looked at my grandfather's face. He's smiling exuberantly, showing no teeth. My mother has often said I resemble him, and in this picture I can see it—the prominent nose, the broad forehead, and the hint of melancholy in his deep-set eyes.

I passed the photo to my cousin.

—*Do you think he was depressed?* I asked.

—*That's how I remember him*, she said. *Not just quiet, but somber.*

Though Alta Faye never spoke directly of the cause of his death, several local newspaper accounts attributed it to suicide. The story made front-page news, and I often wonder if the publicity drew more people to the service than might otherwise have come. I picture the chapel packed full, not an empty seat to be found. I see my parents sitting together in a pew, unable to imagine how something like this could have happened.

PART

THREE

20.

I've said previously that I kept only one letter from my father. That's not exactly true. I also have a xeroxed copy of his suicide note, stored in a folder with the coroner's report, his death certificate, and sympathy cards—things I rarely look at but can't throw away.

Early on, my mother asked me to call the coroner's office and request a copy of the note and the report. Since she, as my father's living spouse, was the only person who could receive the documents, I asked her if I could make an additional copy. Somehow, she permitted me to carry them down the street to a Kinko's. I stood in front of a self-service copy machine, slipping the letter from its envelope. A woman in curlers with a scarf tied around her head stood at a machine across from me. I raised the cover of the copier, and she gave me a weak smile. As I unfolded the letter and laid it flat, I could see in the glass the reflection of my father's words.

The note is addressed to my mother. I sometimes wonder if I should have it in my possession at all. When I think of it now, I often feel disappointed that I'm addressed as an afterthought, as a salutation; saddened by my father's lack of emotion and pedestrian instructions; angry that there was not a second note just for me. But every time I try to imagine throwing it away—burning it,

shredding it, cutting it into a hundred random pieces—
my mind goes blank with paradox. Why should I keep it?
And how can I throw it away?

———

I was surprised to learn that few people who commit
suicide—only about 15 to 25 percent—leave notes. It
may seem unthinkable that someone would deliberately
choose to leave their family, friends, and life itself without saying goodbye. But a person contemplating suicide
is in a decidedly different frame of mind. As psychologist
Thomas Joiner points out, "Most decedents feel alienated
to the point that communication through a note seems
pointless or does not occur to them at all." Indeed, while
"one working hypothesis about writers of suicide notes is
that because they represent a minority of suicides, they
must be different from those suicides who do not leave
notes," most comparative studies have revealed little
difference—beyond note writers merely being "good
correspondents."

"I feel certain I am going mad again," Virginia Woolf
wrote to her husband, "and I shan't recover this time."

"There is nothing new in dying now, though living is
no newer," poet Sergei Yesenin wrote before he hanged
himself in a hotel room.

Woolf's and Yesenin's notes do not set the standard,
however. In general, suicide notes focus on who and what
is being left behind—on the loss that others will experience, on possessions and logistics.

"I am sorry to cause you a lot of trouble and grife [*sic*] but I think this is best for all of us," one man wrote in a note I found collected in famed suicidologist Edwin Shneidman's book *Clues to Suicide*.

"Please take care of my bills," wrote another.

"Take this pen as Helen gave it to me when I went to the army," wrote a third.

The poet Paul Celan underlined a sentence in a biography of Friedrich Hölderlin—"Sometimes this genius goes dark and sinks down into the bitter well of his heart"—and left it open on his desk before he drowned himself in the Seine.

The length of suicide notes varies greatly, but most are short. They tend to be positive about others; to give apologies; to make use of the word *love*. "There's good in all of us," Kurt Cobain wrote, "and I think I simply love people too much. So much that it makes me feel too fucking sad."

A few have been scrawled with crayon, lipstick, or blood. Others are typed cleanly. Others scribbled hurriedly with ink, paint, chalk: often whatever comes to hand easily.

My father's original note lies in the coroner's vault, sealed in a plastic bag. There, his handwriting spreads off the brightness of a canary-yellow page. By contrast, the facsimile is dull with the sheen of copy toner, marked with a coroner's case number. I've only read it a few times. Each time I do, I picture my father writing his final words in a thin ring of lamplight at his desk; walking deliberately down the road to the park, heavy snow filling his shoes; cutting the rope with the cold, sharp edge of a knife. But I always return to the contents of the note: if my father's goodbye displays a certain pragmatic concern for his family—providing advisements and wishes for a future he will take no part in—it's also full of restraint. It doesn't provide motivations for his act or articulate hopes for the world he is leaving behind, bequeathing me with a deep mystery, an almost physical longing to know. I wonder about the secrets it contains; I wonder about its silences and evasions; I wonder about the compulsion to explain, about his need to lay words upon a void.

Over his lifetime, Edwin Shneidman probably read thousands of suicide notes. At the beginning of his career, he believed they might turn out to be the key to understanding suicide. Then, after a decade of study, he realized that most fail to yield the "profound insights" he had hoped for. In the end, he came to assign them a real, if tempered, value: "As a group, suicide notes are neither always psychodynamically rich nor psychodynamically barren, but . . . when the note can be placed within the context of the known details of a life (of which that note is a penultimate part)—*then* words and phrases in the note can take on special meanings, bearing as they do a special freight within that context."

The known details of a life: this is the phrase that sticks with me. What do I really know about my father? There are sharp limits on my understanding. His internal life, like his suicide note, is subject to a score of readings that once deconstructed, can't be put back:

Carolyn—

I have chosen this as the best way to insure that
you, Juliet & Mickey have a decent life.

I am grateful that you have loved me and stayed with
me for 53 years. You are a beautiful & wonderful
woman.

I have chosen to go on the north end of the
footbridge over Montreal Avenue. This is near the
steps I used to exercise on with the Beagles in
Highland Park.

I have left things in the best order I could manage.
I know the timing is not the best—but I was able to live 77
years in really good health and I am grateful for
your care and counsel.

Maybe Juliet will use the Volvo. There is an envelope
in the front flap of the blue notebook on the car
title and also information on the car.

My credit card is on the shelf—I think all automatic
uses have been terminated. There are a few charges pending
for the month—but should be nothing after that.

If she wants to use it the car for a short time that would
work also "a car from the sky" she was waiting for.

The insurance coverage runs thru March—so you could just loan it to her for several months if she really would prefer to sell it.

Please call John at Kroll Ontrack

952-XXX-XXXX

Let them know that I passed away in the night.

Leaving isn't easy. I love you   I love Juliet
       I love Mickey   I love Rachel
           Jim

You'll get a notice in the mail when they renew the CD in the bank.

You can call on the 18th to specify a new renewal term of 7 months

1-800-XXX-XXXX

All my keys are on the shelf. I used the garage door to leave.

Even as I still hope to gather his inner world, every gain is slight. And though I've spent years trying to understand my father's suicide, I have come to think that there can be no simple explanation for a man taking his own life—and that whatever one asserts about another person's psychological experience will be both right and wrong, if it hits the mark at all.

"We do not know our own souls, let alone the souls of others," Virginia Woolf wrote in her famous essay "On Being Ill." "There is a virgin forest, tangled, pathless, in each; a snow field where even the print of birds' feet is unknown."

———

My father, who rarely, if ever, called me, left me a voice-mail the day before he died. He was calling from work, in the late afternoon. Still recuperating from the car accident, asleep and under the influence of pain medication, I didn't hear the phone ring. Had I been awake and seen his name flicker across the screen, I might have answered. Maybe it would have changed the course of events. Or maybe it would have changed my memory of him. But that's not what happened.

—*Hi, Juliet*, he said. *It's Dad. I'm just calling to check on you, to see how you're doing. I'll call you later.*

21.

I know my father is dead, but I don't always remember. Sometimes, darkness pulls and my mind falls blank. Sometimes, his voice calls from somewhere in the future, or from deep in the past. Sometimes, from somewhere I can't identify.

———

A few months after he died, I started dreaming of him all the time. One night: my father, laughing.

   —*I just can't remember him as happy*, I said to Rachel in the morning.

   —*Well, he always seemed happy to see you.*

   —*Really?*

   —*That's the trouble with suicide*, she said. *It eclipses everything.*

———

These dreams ushered in memories, other illusory glimpses that arrived in daytime: my father at the kitchen sink, drinking lemonade from a jar. Or skimming his bread with fat pieces of butter. The faint odor of a clove shampoo he frequently used. How he held a spoon low on the handle, near its dome. He held his razor the same way, fingers wrapped at the base of its head, chin tilting toward the bathroom mirror, a towel draped around his neck. How he organized and arranged things with fastidious care—his desk, his closet, his drawers.

How he was always impeccably groomed. His unvarying wardrobe. In his working years, he wore a suit. Later on, he wore Henley shirts and khakis. He never wore shorts, unless playing tennis; he never wore bright colors or patterns. His shirts were solid navy, white, or black. He often wore a baseball hat absent of logos. He did have a Baltimore Orioles hat—not because he liked the team, but because he liked the bird. And he favored lug sole boots all year long, even in the summer.

The cassette tapes I found in his car: John Adams, Tom Waits, all kinds of country music. When I was a child he liked to play a Herb Alpert & the Tijuana Brass album, *Whipped Cream & Other Delights*, or, at my mother's request, the Moody Blues' *Days of Future Passed*. That was the decade of the Beatles, but we didn't have their music in the house, nor that of the Rolling Stones, Bob Dylan, or Jimi Hendrix. In many ways, my parents were musically out of fashion. This might have later proven a huge disadvantage for me, except that my father made up for the gaps. He regularly bought singles of my favorite radio hits—"Good Vibrations," "Joy to the World," and "To Sir with Love"—which meant that he'd been paying attention to what I loved. We listened to the radio most often in the car, though sometimes I was allowed to tune the living room's transistor and spin the volume high. The most important single I remember was Van Morrison's 1967 "Brown Eyed Girl," which my father miraculously pulled from an elastic pocket inside his briefcase one night after dinner. I watched the record emerge from its white sleeve, the black vinyl glossed in light. The turntable started to spin, the record and the needle both dropped, and then we started to dance. My father wasn't a good singer, and he rarely let it rip. But "Brown Eyed Girl" made magic with him: *Do you remember when we used to sing? Sha la la la la la la la la la la te da.* The song became an anthem we shared. Soon my father had a pet nickname for me: "Brown Eyed Bug." In future renderings, he took the liberty of altering Van Morrison's lyrics. Even now, whenever I hear the song, these are the words I hear.

My first whole memory of him is an image from before I was two. I see the outline of his head in the glimmer of Christmas tree lights. He holds me up, pointing to the tree's sequined star. I feel winged, hovering near the pine, the ceiling almost near enough to touch.

I have a photograph of us taken that year: a good picture of my father. He's thirty-three, young, handsome. He looks relaxed, a slight smile on his face. His right hand is flexed against his outer thigh, a newly gifted stuffed animal (Piglet of Winnie the Pooh) perched nearby. My gaze is fixed on the camera; he's glancing to the left. What does he see? Not my mother, behind the lens. My father's eyes avoid her gaze.

When they were married, my father was twenty-five, my mother just twenty-one. The wedding was in Pittsburg—a small hometown affair. One snapshot, taken from the back balcony of the church, reveals the audience: roughly fifty people, many of the women in hats. My father, dwarfed by the camera's perspective, stands at the front of the church, his arms slack, shoulders slightly slumped. I imagine how, beneath the white tuxedo jacket, a touch too long in the sleeves, his body straightens at the sound of the organ's processional.

His fingers curl inward, and his eyes focus on the boxy shadows cast by floral wreaths onto the carpet. In my mother's hands, a motion-blurred wedding bouquet quivers; she's pulled by her father's arm locked within her elbow. Her father, my grandfather, who in eleven more years will be dead by suicide. My father's father has already been dead by suicide for almost twenty years. Does his own death loom somewhere at the altar? Perhaps where the minister stands, arms wrapped around the Bible, smiling?

My parents were married for just under fifty-three years. They lived most of their life together in the house where I was born, where my mother still lives today. I know little about the early days. My parents didn't talk about themselves. They didn't tell stories. *Your father was in the army*, or *Your father never finished law school*, my mother might say in the course of a random conversation, but that was all. My father never said anything.

I learned more about his past in the process of writing his obituary than I had in all the years of growing up. Rachel volunteered to interview my mother to write the draft, then the three of us edited it together. Though still only a sketch of my father's life, it read for me like a robust history. What did I feel when I saw the draft? How did I react? I know I sat with Rachel and my mother at the dining room table, considering the final price of the obituary, haggling over the cost of each line, but I don't remember the emotions of that evening. Is it too painful to recall? I hadn't heard my mother tell my father's story. I had only the words before us, Rachel's reconstruction of what she'd heard, and there we were cutting it all to the bone, until my father's obituary emerged, a simple skeleton of the original:

> Patterson, James Kennedy "J.K." Age 77, passed away December 17, 2008. He was preceded in death by his parents, the Honorable Edward White Patterson and Leah Kennedy Patterson; and sister, Patricia Shatzkin. He is survived by his wife of 53 years, Carolyn; daughter, Juliet; brother-in-law, Merton Shatzkin and family; cousins; and beloved dog, Mickey. J.K. was a pioneer in the field of computer programming. He worked at IBM, Univac, Northwest Airlines, Quorum and Kroll ON Track. Private family services. Donations may be sent to the Wildlife Rehabilitation Center of Minnesota.

These were the details that fit neatly in the most affordable packaged obituary rate (one photo, ten lines). And since my mother wanted to run notice in both Kansas and Minnesota newspapers over a succession of days, my father's life was truncated to essential facts. As quickly as a story of the man emerged, it disappeared.

My father had thought about being a lawyer. He attended law school at the University of Kansas in Lawrence after my parents were married. It was the first time my mother had lived away from home. I learned from Rachel's interview notes that he dropped out after two years and took a job teaching high school math in New Paltz, New York. My mother went back to school to get her teaching license. They lived in the small town of Millbrook with their dog, Tommy, a rambunctious beagle who once dropped a fully cooked turkey on their doorstep, which they reasoned must have been cooling on a neighbor's windowsill. It was Tommy who jump-started their thirty-year love affair with beagles: when my parents went on to breed, rear, and show them, it was under the kennel name of "Millbrook."

In 1963, the year I was born, they moved to Minnesota. My father began his job at Sperry UNIVAC. My mother was already pregnant. The position must have been an enormous opportunity: UNIVAC was the first business computer on the market. To the general public, "UNIVAC" literally meant "computer." And it was a lucrative industry. The cost of a UNIVAC 1100 in the 1960s could run into the millions of dollars. A new Buick Riviera cost $4,333.

In his first years at the company, my father worked as an on-site programmer, helping to install and code systems for clients. To secure the job, he had to apply for a high-level government security clearance; he never revealed why, exactly, but my mother suspects that Sperry UNIVAC may have had a contract with the Department of Defense. He traveled often, working with government agencies and large companies across the world, including Australia, Japan, Germany, Canada, France, and England. And he usually brought home souvenirs from these places: a boomerang, a paper fan, a T-shirt, a carved wooden beaver for my nightstand.

Before he left on these trips, he always left a note or a card on the floor near my bed. When I was older, he used a Lite-Brite toy, creating illuminated messages out of colored pegs to glow in the corner of my room: *Be good, I love you. See you soon.*

One more dreamlike memory: from my father's office chair, the perfect view of a robin's nest erected in low-lying shrubs just outside the window. I was twelve years old. The nest was an open cup of grass and twigs held together with mud. For several days, my father had watched its construction, each night at the dinner table reporting on its progress with fascination and exuberance. In the two weeks of the brood's incubation, he and I made several trips to his office to watch the nest's progression. It was a rather unlikely place for anything wild to take hold.

My father worked in an office park near the airport, and nothing but freeways and concrete structures surrounded his building. In fact, his windows faced a parking lot, and with the exception of some token landscaping, there was little to admire by way of beauty.

Three eggs hatched a day apart. We watched the last chick fight its way out of the shell, and when the bird finally emerged, the mother threw the now-empty shell out of the nest. The birds grew quickly, fledged in a few weeks, and learned to fly on the small strip of lawn outside the office. When the brood left for the season, we carefully removed the nest and brought it home. My mother had a collection of sorts: nests of various sizes cataloged and housed in the garage. Her penchant for preserving natural artifacts may have begun when she was a kindergarten teacher. Her classroom had resembled a natural history museum, filled with rudimentary dioramas that she used in her lesson plans. The habit was passed on to me: today, my bookshelves are covered with rocks, driftwood, and nests.

22.

Three days after my father's death, snow fell. I stood in my kitchen watching it blanket the roof of the garage, a line from E. E. Cummings—"the snow doesn't give a soft white / damn Whom it touches"—filling my head. Friends had gathered for a makeshift wake at the house, and some of them were milling about a table of food nearby. Most everyone had brought something in a gesture of sympathy; the kitchen was cluttered with flowers, food, desserts, and bottles of wine. It looked something like a party, but it was nothing like a party. Though relieved to be in the company of those I loved, I felt numb and shocked. I remember only silence—snow falling, my father trudging knee-deep across my mind's eye—but I know that isn't true. I must have spoken. Indeed, in the days that followed, I found myself repeatedly talking about what had happened. Looking back, I can see that the pressure I felt to explain was instinctual, a means of survival. I had watched my parents remain silent on the subject. For me, now, it seemed as though I could talk about nothing else.

Soon friends began avoiding me or altogether disappeared. The few who remained either changed the subject when I started talking or offered unhelpful advice: *You've got to move on with your life, put this behind you. Haven't you grieved enough already?* It seemed as though they wanted me to preserve the silence around the issue of suicide that I'd unintentionally kept my whole life. One friend suggested I purchase a teddy bear for solace, and another—failing to remember my car accident and the associated pain that still radiated through my body—suggested exercise. And still another asked my permission to solicit a shamanistic healer to contact my father in the beyond, which I gave unwittingly. I soon regretted my carelessness. The healer began emailing long and detailed accounts of my father's existence in a realm between this world and the next. I was either unwilling or unable to believe any of these efforts were in good faith, even though the friend who brokered the healer's services assured me good things would come of it. A few days later, the healer's last email arrived. *He's crossed over,* she wrote. *His journey is complete. But I'm sorry, there's no message for you. He seemed unwilling to talk.* I didn't know whether to cry or to laugh at this news. I really had no use for this information, and yet I felt desperate for something material, something that would ease the loss.

Then, winter stalled time to a grinding halt. I felt suspended in a timeless state of nothingness; one day became indistinguishable from the next. Medical appointments were all that anchored me: many afternoons were crowded with visits to the chiropractor, massage therapist, and physical therapist. The physical therapist's office was a maze of small examination rooms and one larger room containing scales, ergometers, straps, tubes, balls, and strengthening machines. During most of my appointments, I spent my time lying on a mechanical traction table designed to stretch muscles and joints around my neck, relieving the pressure of compressed nerves in the spinal canal. The table was upholstered in blue vinyl and housed in a private room empty of all other equipment and furnishings. I would lie on my back and stare at the blank walls as the therapist strapped a harness around my head and chin. The harness was attached to a track and pulley system automated by a small machine that protruded from a white steel bar above the head of the table like a bulky eye. Once the harness had been adjusted and the settings on the machine selected, the therapist left the room and closed the door. I lay in the darkness of nothing: no sound, no touch but for the strap under my chin, tugging. I felt relieved and then, as the weeks passed, more afraid, disturbed by both my injury and my treatment, the apparatus of the machine, the harness around my head like a snare. I felt a growing sense of unease in my body, chasing the dead.

I tried to be a good partner, a good employee, and a good patient. But I felt terribly alone and withdrawn. Self-pitying. I was plagued by surges of panic and grief that overwhelmed my thinking. Why had my father taken his own life? Could I have prevented it?

I began to have nightmares that kept me awake all hours of the night. My father no longer appeared in my dreams. Instead, objects vanished, went up in smoke. Parts of my body—arms and teeth—fell off or disintegrated. Sometimes, I found myself at an edge, cutting with knives, stringing a rope. And with each dream, a new turn of loneliness and fear.

Reading was one way I tried to occupy my mind, to avoid the worst of its wild, tidal swings, and in the books I read, I learned that my isolation was a normal consequence of grief associated with suicide. The suicide bereaved, I was told, must not only attempt to cope with the death of someone close to them, but frequently must also do so in a context of stigma, shame, guilt, and confusion.

In the season of my father's death, books massed in piles on the floor. I wanted answers. I wanted to understand not just bereavement, but suicide itself. Who dies by suicide? And why? Wasn't it helpful to know that the grief of a suicide is unique? That suicide was more common than murder in the United States? That I wasn't alone in my grief? That nightmares were common? That relationships become frequently strained in the wake of the death? Not really. But still, I kept reading.

I read and reread the few documents my father had left behind, scoured the Internet for my paternal grandfather, then read articles and journals and more books on suicide. Some of the reading was difficult, fueled bleak imaginings and filled my head with apocalyptic bits of information and strange facts. I wrote these all down in list form, making a taxonomy of my apprehensions. That list, when I look at it now, is stark:

According to the Centers for Disease Control and Prevention, suicide takes the lives of more than 47,500 Americans every year. There is one death by suicide every eleven minutes; on average, 130 suicides a day. Men die by suicide three and a half times more often than women. For every suicide, there's an estimated 29 attempts. You are two times more likely to commit suicide in the United States than be murdered by someone else; suicide is the tenth leading cause of death in the United States. For every suicide, six deeply affected survivors are left behind. Each year, roughly 285,000 people become suicide survivors. Suicide rates are highest in the spring; Christmas season is actually below average. Most people who die by their own hand die on a Sunday, Monday, or Tuesday. Suicides are less frequent as the week progresses. A majority of people are stone-cold sober when they die by suicide, though a high percentage of people who die by suicide have a long history of substance abuse. Using the government's demographic classifications, the highest suicide rates in the country are among whites, American Indians, and Alaska Natives. Suicide rates are also high among vulnerable groups such as refugees and migrants; lesbian, gay, bisexual, transgender, and intersex individuals; and incarcerated people. Established artists and writers, particularly poets, are more likely to commit suicide than the general population. From 1999 to 2019, the total suicide rate increased 33 percent. And according to the World Health Organization, "While the link between suicide and mental disorders (in particular, depression and alcohol use disorders) is well established in high-income countries, many suicides happen impulsively in moments of crisis . . . such as financial problems, relationship break-up, or chronic pain and illness." Children of parents who kill themselves are at a higher risk to commit suicide later in life.

———

These facts aren't immaterial, but looking at this list now I can see how little this information helped me to know or access my sorrow. Instead, it was the literary forms of solace I turned to that granted me passage to my feelings, by way of voice.

"No one ever told me that grief felt so like fear," C. S. Lewis wrote in *A Grief Observed*, published after the death of his wife. These words come to me now, looking over the notebooks I filled so many years ago.

A Grief Observed was one of the few books that seemed to make some sense of my experience: grief not only as sadness but also as terror. "When I speak of fear, I mean . . . the recoil of the organism from its destruction; the smothery feeling; the sense of being a rat in a trap," wrote Lewis, an image I'd hold in my mind as a figure and description of grief. *I feel like a rabbit caught in a snare* was a phrase I sometimes used, should anyone ask how I was doing.

Most of what I read was too simple or prescriptive or written without the force of language, but there were other exceptions. A. Alvarez's *The Savage God*, which approached suicide from a literary perspective. George Howe Colt's *November of the Soul*, a wide-ranging book incorporating extensive interviews and case studies, and Kay Redfield Jamison's *Night Falls Fast*, a scientific and historical exploration of the subject. Above all, however, my notebooks quote from the work of one man: Edwin Shneidman, the psychologist who studied suicide notes. Nearly everything I read made mention of him. A pioneer in the study and prevention of suicide, he viewed it as a psychological crisis and quoted Albert Camus often in describing it as the "one truly serious philosophical problem." He believed suffering was at the heart of suicide, which he described as "psychache."

This one central idea resonated for me in thinking about my father's—and later both my grandfathers'—suicides. To even attempt to make sense of their deaths, I had to piece a lot of things together. The mystery was moored in history and facts. But underneath it all was psychological pain. I had intuited this before reading Shneidman, but the way he demonstrated his thesis, with the fugitive thinking of a poet, somehow made it much clearer for me.

Shneidman died at the age of ninety-one, on the day we buried my father: May 15, 2009. At that point, I knew very little about his life. A few months previous, I'd encountered a profile of him in the *Los Angeles Times*, where he told the story of a fairly recent near-death experience. His blood pressure had been skyrocketing. He told the reporter that "as he lay in the back of the ambulance, he stared through the transparent ceiling at the sky and watched the world pass by. He expected everything to go dark, and when they pulled into the bay of the UCLA Medical Center, he started to cry, knowing that the doctors would save him." I'd read only one of his books when he died, but he already felt like an intimate, a trusted friend. The profile mentioned how very common this feeling was; when Shneidman was alive, "the stream of visitors to his house [was] nearly constant."

Shortly after I returned home from Pittsburg, I found an accompanying video slideshow about Shneidman on the *Los Angeles Times*'s website. I must have watched it more than two dozen times. Many of those times, I wept. I can't say why.

I know the exact sequence of images: first, a still portrait of Shneidman in a lawn chair, wearing a tweed suit coat, one of his ubiquitous whale-printed ties, and a pair of striped pajama bottoms. Fade: blackness, the sound of his labored breath. A new image emerges: Shneidman slumped in the same chair, legs crossed, feet thrust forward, hand covering his face. Fixed in the frame's edge: the backyard, a statue of the Venus Genetrix. Then his voice, speaking to the reporter and photographer who had been visiting him for weeks: "I was saddened today by something that you two could not have known, and for a moment I was startled at the deterioration of the statue. I hadn't seen it in months, and all of a sudden it's falling apart. And it's a paradigm of me—I'm that old statue."

The backyard: an avocado tree, a ginger plant, and the Venus, her chipped knees and moss-covered feet. Fade. A sequence of household objects: a red folding clock; electric cords strewn across the carpet; a white toaster, abandoned toast still lingering inside. Fade. Shneidman's legs dangling over the edge of his bed, his shins exposed between the hem of black trousers and rim of black socks; Shneidman reading in bed, his face cast in the chiaroscuro of California light; a metal-framed walker pitched on the lawn. Fade. More shots of his home, and finally, getting dressed for his portrait: he knots a navy-blue tie, a sea of red whales spouting white air. Fade.

Born in Pennsylvania to Jewish immigrants, Shneidman was raised and lived most of his adult life in Los Angeles. He studied psychology at UCLA, entering the undergraduate program at the age of sixteen and earning a master's degree before serving in the Army Air Force during World War II. When the war ended, he returned to school and pursued a doctorate in clinical psychology. As an intern, he studied the potential environmental causes of schizophrenia at a VA hospital, searching for his place in the field of psychology. A path came into view in 1949, when he was asked to write condolence letters to the families of two veterans who had died by suicide. He researched the cases at the Los Angeles coroner's office, and as he searched the records for more information about the men, he discovered hundreds of suicide notes hidden away in the files.

After a day-long immersion examining notes, Shneidman contacted his friend and fellow VA trainee Norman Farberow and told him about the discovery. Farberow had focused his PhD on suicide attempts. With a supply of 721 notes "borrowed" (as Shneidman later confessed) from the vault, the two men hoped to unlock the secret to understanding suicide. They approached nonsuicidal people to write a control group of fake notes, then formatted both sets of notes on index cards, randomized them, and compared them. In that moment, contemporary suicidology was born.

"We believed (with excessive optimism) that, like Freud's notion about dreams being the royal road to the unconscious, suicide notes might prove to be the royal road to the understanding of suicidal phenomena," Shneidman wrote in *Autopsy of a Suicidal Mind*. As I have mentioned previously, the notes turned out to be disappointingly mundane; the royal road led to a dead end. But, working together, Shneidman and Farberow continued to expand the study of suicide.

In 1958, the two men teamed up with psychiatrist Robert Litman to help found the Los Angeles Suicide Prevention Center, establishing the first such institution in the country. Together, they conceived the idea of "lethality," which Shneidman defined as "the probability of a specific individual's killing himself . . . in the immediate future." Their Suicide Potential Rating Scale, a questionnaire that assesses lethality, is still used today. They also identified the "suicidal crisis," theorizing that people are generally acutely suicidal only during a brief window. And at the request of the coroner's office, they created the "psychological autopsy," based on conversations with those close to a victim, to more conclusively establish whether a death was actually a suicide or not. Their proximity to Hollywood brought them their most famous case: Marilyn Monroe.

They declared Monroe's sudden death a suicide, citing evidence to suggest that she suffered from suicidal depression. She had overdosed on barbiturates, drugs that one must take in large quantities to be fatal, which indicated clear intent. Her psychological autopsy was never made public, but the publicity surrounding her case helped thrust Shneidman, Farberow, and Litman into the national limelight. Their psychological autopsy procedure was widely adopted as Farberow enlisted other researchers in developing it further. Shneidman left the Los Angeles center in 1966 and organized a national suicide-prevention project through the National Institutes of Health (NIH), and, in just few years, established prevention centers across the country.

After his work with the NIH, he became a professor of thanatology—the study of death—at UCLA, where he taught seminars on suicide and Herman Melville. He began to apply his theories to the author's life and work, including, in 1973, a psychological autopsy on the death of Melville's son Malcolm. Malcolm Melville died in 1867, but the case was presented to Shneidman's staff as contemporary, coming from the coroner's office. "The facts were presented as close to the historical record as information from solid biographical sources could provide," Shneidman wrote later. "Malcolm had a deep unconscious feeling of not being wanted by his father; that it would be better if he were out of the way, dead. On the morning of his death, the choice for Malcolm was between the memory of his mother's kiss a few hours before and the terror of (and the need to protect himself against) his father's rage to come."

According to his death certificate, Malcolm died at age eighteen from a "pistol shot wound in [his] right temporal region." The official attribution changed from suicide, to accident, to death while of unsound mind. "Historically," Shneidman wrote, "the mode of his death has remained equivocal." The consensus among his group, however, was that Malcolm's death was likely a suicide. "The sum and substance of my speculations is that, psychologically, the groundwork for Malcolm's self-destructive behavior was laid in the first 2 years of his life," he wrote. "The basic unconscious charge to the boy from his father was that Malcolm should not get in the way, should not grow up, should not live out his own life. From the beginning, it would be better for his father if he, Malcolm, were simply not around the house. The first 2 years of life were 'Shadows present, foreshadowing deeper shadows to come.'"

These last words, a quote from Herman Melville's novella *Benito Cereno*, I underlined in my notes. No one talks or writes about suicide the way Shneidman does. He was a bibliophile. A lover of classical music. A man who relied on language and metaphor: he didn't just openly discuss what had been unspeakable in my family, but put it in a context that made sense to me. He wasn't prescriptive; he was literary, a surrogate father, a good father. I'd thought I was chasing answers, understanding, as I read, but it was my father I was chasing—my father I saw as I wept, watching Shneidman on screen; the father I might have had, as he looked courageously at death and did not turn away, and made me feel that I might too.

23.

I hated music after my father died. I had never really liked Christmas carols in the first place, but that winter I was reminded of how unavoidable they are. It felt unbearable to tolerate their jolliness when an unending territory of grief expanded before me. Music had become bothersome, if not painful, to my nervous system. I made a conscious decision to avoid it as much as possible.

This all temporarily changed a few months short of the first anniversary of his death, when I was admitted to the hospital with a bowel obstruction, often a symptom of advanced colon cancer. After a battery of tests and images, doctors ruled out the colon as the source. But the possibility of cancer still loomed. An MRI revealed a mass under my uterus, in the cavity strangely named the "cul-de-sac." *I don't like the looks of this*, one surgeon warned. Another pronounced that I likely had no more than a few months to live.

The night before a scheduled exploratory surgery, facing the possibility of my own death, I broke my fast with music and listened to the classical composer John Adams from my hospital bed. Visiting hours were over. Rachel had already gone home. I was alone in the room after a nurse had once again taken my vitals. In a couple periods of his life, my father had listened to Adams obsessively;

my choice was a deliberate one. I slipped on headphones and faced the darkened window near my bed, listening to *Common Tones in Simple Time*, a minimalist piece that Adams once said conveys the feeling of "viewing the surface of a continent from the window of a jet plane." I closed my eyes and flew.

—*The first thing we'll do is biopsy the tissue*, my surgeon explained to Rachel and my mother the next day, as I lay on a gurney outside the operating room. *If it looks bad, we won't do much. If I'm not back out here in the hallway in an hour, that's good news.*

A nurse came to give me a sedative. I felt the sting of the needle striking my vein, and death drifted into my mind. I wasn't afraid. Maybe I was already, in some way, dead. Or maybe the anxiety I might have felt was subsumed by my anguish about my father. As the sedative took hold, I thought of Rachel, three months into a second pregnancy, and tried to fix her features in my mind.

The subject of a baby had reemerged several months after Rachel's miscarriage. She was eager to try again. And although I had once been resistant and even unwelcoming to the idea, especially in the immediate aftermath of my father's death, something had changed—I was still preoccupied with unearthing my ancestral past, still mired in grief, but I had begun to feel that having a child made sense in the balance of things, and after the last year, Rachel's joy and enthusiasm at the idea were catching. We decided to schedule another insemination, assuming it would take more than one try. It didn't. It was hard not to see the ease of this as providence, as a sublime corrective measure, as a way forward.

Now, as I was wheeled into surgery, I imagined Rachel somewhere nearby in the hospital waiting room and held on to that idea, yielding to the future.

The mass was benign: not cancer, but a form of endometriosis more invasive than the doctors expected. Tissue normally found inside the uterus had spread outside, gathering in the cul-de-sac and beyond. Tendrils gathered at my ovaries, wrapped my colon, and trailed up my urethra to the edge of my bladder. Three surgeons cut and scraped tissue from my body, then repaired the colon and the urethra in a five-and-a-half-hour surgery.

The cause of endometriosis isn't known. You can't have your blood, urine, or saliva tested to confirm its presence. The only way to verify it is to undergo diagnostic surgery, which explained why I'd been taken to such extremes medically. My doctors surmised I'd had the disease most of my adult life.

—*But I'm guessing,* my surgeon said, a few weeks later, *that there's been an accelerated growth in the last year or two. We may never know why.*

We were in a small examination room for a post-surgical consultation. She was seated on a wheeled stool next to the examination table where I sat, legs dangling over the edge, dressed in a hospital gown.

—*Could be genetic, could be hormonal,* she continued, as she flipped through the pages of my file. *Could also have been induced by the stress of recovery from the car accident. There's some evidence to suggest that exposure to stress can worsen endometriosis.*

I hadn't told her about my father's suicide, nor did that information appear in my medical file; it hadn't seemed relevant. But after the appointment, I began to wonder how the event might have had a deeper impact on my overall physical health. I already knew about some of grief's effects on the body—anxiety, loss of appetite, lack of sleep—because I had experienced them. But, although it now seemed obvious, I hadn't considered the possible connections between the stress of grieving and disease.

In the months following my surgery, back in the familiar territory of recovery (pain medications, sleep, long hours in bed), I returned to reading. I learned that the links between grief and physical health are well established. Your nervous system becomes highly stimulated; immunity weakens; biological rhythms are disturbed; metabolism and circulation change. If you already have an existing chronic health challenge, it may become worse. And if you don't, there are numerous physical diseases that have been directly linked to stress and inflammation, which grief can cause. Here's just a partial list: cardiovascular disorders, cancer, pneumonia, diabetes, influenza, and glaucoma. There are also myriad threats to mental health, including post-traumatic stress disorder, anxiety, suicidal ideation, and depression.

Though it's hard to determine how many of us actually become sick as a result of grief, research has shown that if we do, the majority of us will experience illness in the first six months following a loved one's death. There will likely be decisive correlations between our emotive descriptions of grief and the physical symptoms manifested in the body: *I felt as if I'd been hit in the stomach, my stomach was in knots, I felt as though I'd been disemboweled.*

"There are essentially only two kinds of mourning and grief," Edwin Shneidman wrote early in his career. "Those which accrue to deaths from heart, cancer, accident, disaster and the like, and those which relate to the stigmatizing death of a loved one by suicide."

He was the first to use the term "suicide-victim," acknowledging the impact "suicide can have on those left behind." He described the relationship in this way: "The person who commits suicide puts his psychological skeleton in the survivor's emotional closet—he sentences the survivor to a complex of negative feelings and, most importantly, to obsessing about the reasons for the suicide death."

In *SOS: A Handbook for Survivors of Suicide*, a pamphlet I was given after my father's death, the word "survivor" carried both practical and metaphoric applications: "The American Psychiatric Association ranks the trauma of losing a loved one to suicide as 'catastrophic'—on par with that of a concentration camp experience." Late in life, Shneidman wondered if it was possible to formulate a guiding principle for a good death, an approach that keeps these survivors in mind. "I would offer, as a beginning, the following Golden Rule for the dying scene: Do unto others *as little as possible.* . . . Have your dying be a courtly death, among the best things that you ever did."

24.

One morning, when it felt like my obsessive research had temporarily come to a stop, I dug out the folder from my father's desk, the one that contained the newspaper clippings about Edward. It had been sitting in a box in the closet, and now I finally married its content to my own file. I was alone in my study, seated on the floor with the door pulled shut. Sun fell on the rug and rimmed the opposite wall. My research folder was stuffed with notes and materials from my many trips to Pittsburg: interviews I'd conducted, scribbled-upon scraps of paper, and notebooks where I'd composed the earliest sentences of this book; family photographs, newspaper clippings, and census records; and academic articles on suicide, trauma, and history. As I wove my father's notes and clippings into my own, I was reminded once more that he and I had traveled the same path—me puzzling over his death just as he had puzzled over his own father's and my following the bread crumbs of his research to Edward.

Where had that search taken me? If I was a detective, I'd discovered many potential motives, but these generated more questions than answers:

All of my forebears had a troubled relationship with masculinity. Each of them, in their own ways, were driven and burdened by the idealism of being a man.

They belonged to a culture of individualism and separation. They kept themselves too apart. "Ideals are brutal," Kathryn Bond Stockton writes in her book *Gender(s)*. "You can't help but fail them, since they are ideal. That is, not real. If the ideal you fail, moreover, is the ideal that 'you must not fail'—*this* is masculinity—you are going to be a failure, with consequences for everyone, including you." Some of them took significant financial, professional, and personal risks. Edward had lost his political career, cheated on his wife, flirted with divorce. Both he and my father may have gambled—Edward for leisure and my father on the stock market. How do you provide for others when risks don't pay off? Life insurance. Meticulous preparations. A misguided sense of caretaking. Some of them were ill. Do you burden others with your pain? No. If you're William or my father, you stay silent. You refuse treatment. You seek your own counsel. My father, who had refused his required heart valve replacement, faced a terminal prognosis. Statistically speaking, terminal illness is not a large driver of suicide, but what did it mean to look death in the face and to speak of it to no one?

And what about mental illness? There's wide consensus that at least 90 percent of suicide decedents in Western countries experience a mental disorder at the time of death. People with bipolar disorder, for example, are at a much higher risk for suicide than the general population. William was, by his own description, depressed at the end of his life. Given Edward's paranoia (drawing the shades, never sitting near a window or with his back to the door), rageful temper, and alcohol abuse, it's possible he suffered from an undiagnosed mood disorder.

There was also the thing that had been lurking at the edge of my mind—genetics. The causes and predictors of suicide can't be fully determined. There are all sorts of risk factors; there's no royal road. Even so, "around 43 percent of the variability in suicidal behavior among the general population can be explained by genetics," psychologist Jesse Bering reports in his book *Suicidal: Why We Kill Ourselves.* And a considerable part of how a person might develop the capability for suicide is also genetic, according to Thomas Joiner. As I have mentioned previously, Joiner's theory of suicide centers on three factors, one of which is transitioning from desire for death into action. In his view, it's actually very hard to make this leap. And according to him, about 40 percent of the variable of this trait is genetic. "The rest of it," he thinks, "has to do with . . . learned experiences of having faced fear and physical pain": "experiences of injury, maybe violence or abuse. Occupational factors can come into play if the work is very physical, for example if it's very rugged."

According to the young and controversial science of epigenetics, as Benedict Carey writes in the *New York Times,* "trauma can leave a chemical mark on a person's genes, which then is passed down to subsequent generations." On the floor of my study, I thought about what Edward had passed on to my father—an appetite for risk, a lasting loss, and perhaps, ultimately, suicidal capability. I thought about fear and physical pain and my car accident and my experience with endometriosis. I thought about what these men had shared with each other and with me. "The idea that we carry some biological trace of our ancestors' pain has a strong emotional appeal," Carey writes. It certainly did for me. What pain did these men bequeath to one another?

Finally, in coming to know my grandfathers, I'd expanded the circle to environment. Pittsburg: with its unfettered industrial revolution; its electric relays and steam engines; and its long suffering during the Depression. With its booming and declining industries. With its labor disputes and the men and women on either side of them. With its ethnic violence. With its denuded landscape. With its flooded pits that men disappear into. With its sinkholes. But could any of this amount to more than suggestion?

Yes and no. Where in the beginning of my search I had felt like an exile with little to measure myself by, I now felt as though I knew something more about my personal suicides—about my father and grandfathers. I knew more about them as men. And I knew more about the place from which they all had come.

And did Pittsburg have anything to do with this legacy? Again, yes and no. These investigations hadn't yielded any more certainty, nor revealed (as I had sometimes hoped) clear motivations, but everything felt implicated. Looking at the evidence spread out before me, what I started to see was that the void of these three suicides could never resolve—that it would keep spreading, keep eating up the story and the ground under my feet, so that nothing would ever be totally clear.

Even if Pittsburg couldn't provide any definite answers, I kept returning to it, and to my family history. In early 2012, I arranged a visit with my uncle Merton in Kansas City. I hadn't seen him since my father's memorial service. I could count on one hand the number of times I had ever seen him, even though he was married to my father's sister, Pat, for more than forty years. My father and his sister had had a difficult relationship, and as adults were estranged for reasons that no one could seem to explain. When I asked Merton if something in particular had happened, he said, *I've never understood it. Maybe they just didn't like each other.* But then he added that *Pat had been put out* by my father's absence in the care of his mother in her later years, especially as her memory declined. She was angry that my father never bothered to visit Leah once Merton and Pat moved her to a long-term care facility near their home.

Merton and Pat spent a few years of their married life in Pittsburg, then moved to Kansas City the year I was born. Family gatherings were already the exception, not the rule. Pat died in 2003, but I didn't attend her funeral; when Merton slipped under the tent at my father's memorial service, I hadn't seen him in more than thirty years. I didn't recognize him until he removed his hat and greeted my mother with an embrace. He was in his eighties, with thinning hair and skin marbled from the sun. But he still moved with the physical confidence of a younger man, and his face exuded kindness. He smiled as he seated himself in an empty row of folding chairs and gave me a little familiar wave, as though we'd recently been in contact. There were just a few guests in attendance, most of whom I didn't know or was meeting for the first time: some of my mother's distant relatives; a friend of my father's from high school, who'd shown up after seeing the obituary in the local paper. My aunt Rosemary, along with Krista and her three children, filled the small section of chairs reserved for family. Earlier that day, I had picked Rachel up at the Kansas City airport and driven her to Pittsburg. It was a relief to have her there.

At a luncheon in the Mall Deli following the service, I sat next to Merton and began to fill his ears with details of Edward's archives. He took an immediate interest. Like my cousin, he'd made a hobby of compiling genealogical records, and I'd soon discover that although he was only a Patterson by marriage, he'd long been absorbed in unearthing our family's history. A few days later, he emailed me a color-coded spreadsheet of a family tree he'd spent years constructing and mentioned that he'd found a box of photographs in his basement, retrieved from Leah's house after she moved to the care facility.

Now, three years later, he greeted me at his front door with a handshake, and then ushered me in. The small house was crammed with antiques and artifacts, things Pat began collecting late in her life. Though it had been nearly ten years since her death, there were photographs of her everywhere: on chairs and table-tops, across the seats of a couch, propped against the edge of a bathroom sink. There were photographs of her as a child, as a young woman, and at the end of her life. I was moved by the sheer excess of her image. Another complete and utter stranger, a strikingly beautiful woman who, in her later years, began to look very much like my grandmother and, in distant ways, my father.

    —*I can't bear to take them down, but I know I need to*, he said, leading me into the living room. The box he'd mentioned was sitting on a card table. *This is everything I have. I'm afraid some of it hasn't been stored very well.*

He left the room to make tea.

On the other side of the room was a photograph of Edward as a young man, dressed in an army field jacket. His eyes were remote, inscrutable. This was a man I still didn't know.

    —*Did you see this one of your grandfather?* Merton asked as he entered the room, gesturing with a teacup. *It's a beautiful shot.*

    —*Yes*, I said.

He set down the cup on the table and sat in a flimsy folding chair beside me.

    —*What have you found in the box?*

Absently, I scattered photographs across the table.

    —*Oh, these are pictures from the Kennedy family reunion*, he said. *Your grandmother and her siblings.*

In the photographs, Leah appears much as I remember her: a sturdy woman with a shock of luxurious hair. I knew her only after that hair had gone white, lifting away from her forehead in a great expanse. She was heavy-set, with imposing shoulders and ponderous arms. She always wore a dress and proper shoes, even around the house. She had simple but elegant taste, and her clothes gave off an air of wealth and refinement, even though she was actually a woman of frugal means.

But she was also an eccentric and unceremonious person, especially in later years, when she seemed to become more and more oblivious to the world around her. Eventually I understood this behavior as the early signs of Alzheimer's. As a child, I called her "Silly Grandma," a name that underscored her trifling nature; in stark contrast to my mother's mother, she was an ideal child's companion, indulgent and charming. She loved to take afternoon drives through town in her car, with no other purpose than our enjoying the pleasure of each other's company and relishing the full personality of her 1958 Edsel Ranger, which frequently backfired on acceleration, prompting my grandmother to wave her hand in the air and laugh. Rather than having the car repaired, she accepted its condition, affectionately christening it "Chitty Chitty Bang Bang." As a child, I was delighted by the thrill of each small explosion, my grandmother laughing as the car bucked violently forward in a cloud of smoke and noise bursting from the tailpipe.

Now there she was standing among her three sisters and their husbands, posed near a banquet table burdened with large platters of food, a thin smile crossing her face. There were dozens of copies of this picture in the box. The utter repetition of the image was dramatic, but even more striking was the fact that this one fat envelope made up nearly a third of the entire box. The remaining photos presented a scant portrait of my father's early life. What was there: photos of various houses, cars, and the family dog; my father's high school graduation photo, pictures of Leah as a young woman, a photograph of my father and his sister in Washington, DC; snapshots of political lawn signs, garden beds, headstones. What was missing: family portraits, photos of my grandparents' wedding, pictures of my father as a baby.

—*Is this everything?* I asked Merton as he took another envelope from the box. It was hard to believe there weren't more artifacts. Where had everything gone?

—*Yes*, he said.

—*No other pictures?*

—*Not that I know of.*

Merton set the envelope on the table. Gradually, he took the remaining objects out of the box. A few stray birthday cards, gold-leafed invitations to presidential dinners, a letter my grandfather had written while stationed in France during World War I, a title deed to the house, and some of Leah's writing, including a small personality sketch she wrote of Huey Long, Louisiana's radically populist governor, a friend of Edward's when he served in the House.

A few newspaper clippings came out next. There were two articles from the *Pittsburg Headlight* recounting the circumstances of my grandfather's death—the same accounts my father had found and copied at the library. And there was one additional clipping from the *Columbus (KS) Daily Advocate*:

> **A note written to his wife by E. W. Patterson of Pittsburg, former member of Congress and supervisor of district No. 3 for the 1940 federal census was the outstanding evidence**

indicating Patterson had committed suicide sometime early yesterday, investigating authorities reported.

Patterson's body was found . . . slumped over in the front seat of the ex-congressman's motor car near Weir about 1:30 o'clock yesterday afternoon. There was a bullet hole in the right temple and a .45 caliber automatic pistol, identified as Patterson's was tightly clenched in his hand.

The only suspicious circumstance discovered by the investigators so far was the presence of three empty cartridge shells on the floor of the car, automatically ejected from the pistol after it had been fired. Sheriff Clarence Burger stated that there were no bullet holes found in the auto.

A coroner's jury was sworn in and taken to view the body about 6 o'clock yesterday afternoon. County Attorney Joe Henbest announced that an inquest would be held "as soon as all the evidence is assembled" but the time had not been definitely set. "There are indications of suicide," Mr. Henbest said, "but we're not sure yet that it was."

Mr. Patterson left Pittsburg shortly before noon Wednesday on a 2-day trip in connection with the federal business census.

Frank and Bill White, who are said to live north of the place where the body was found, told Sheriff Burger that they noticed Patterson's car parked alongside the road about 5 p.m. Wednesday. They made two trips past the machine, they said. The first time the car door was closed and the second time it was open, according to the sheriff. It was also reported that the right rear tire was flat.

Mr. Henbest has revealed that investigators have not disclosed any indications of foul play. There was about $15 in cash in Patterson's pockets and his watch was on his person, still running. His dog was waiting outside the car.

The note addressed to his wife was found on the steering wheel splattered with blood. On the floor of the car was a picture of his son James, dressed in a cowboy suit.

Finally, Merton removed a staple-bound pamphlet titled *Personal Property*, embossed with a rubber ink stamp from an insurance company. Inside, on the book's blank pages, my grandmother had carefully noted family possessions, the end of the list trailing off in pencil: *cherry breakfast set, walnut frame mirror, .45 Colt Automatic Government Model, pen and pencil flashlight, one electric heater.*

Several hours had passed since I arrived, the sun was lower in the sky, and the light through the curtains had become fuller and somehow began to make everything in the room seem darker. I thought about the two-hour drive back to Pittsburg, which I didn't want to make at night, and started to collect and carefully replace the contents of the box.

—*Finished?* Merton asked.

—*I think so. For now.*

—*I'm sorry there wasn't more*, he said, removing our empty cups from the table. *If there's anything you want, I'd be happy to copy it for you.*

—*Thank you.*

Merton walked back to the kitchen to rinse our dishes. I selected a few photographs and newspaper articles and set them aside.

—*It's nice that you're taking an interest in the family history*, he said, returning to the living room. *My children seem to have no interest at all.*

—*Can I leave you some money for postage?*

—*No, no. I'm happy to do it.*

As I walked to the front door, Merton paused.

—*One more thing. I almost forgot.* He stepped into the dining room and picked up two bound manuscripts from the table. *I think you should have them*, Merton said. *I have two copies. This set was intended for your father.* He flipped open the cover of one book and pointed to a penned inscription.

The books were a genealogical record of the Patterson family that my great-aunt, Belle Patterson Rush—Edward's sister—had assembled. Bound in cream-colored folders with brass fasteners, the manuscripts were slightly worn and smooth to the touch. Belle had marked each clearly in her careful script and added the date, *August 1958*, above my father's name. He would have been twenty-seven years old then, married just two years, still living in Lawrence, Kansas, and enrolled in law school. I'm not sure he ever received the gift. Belle might have delivered them to Leah to pass along; maybe she forgot about them or maybe my father never bothered to pick up his copy. How else would they both have fallen into Merton's hands?

It was Belle's manuscript that would allow me, ultimately, to reconstruct my great-grandfather William Lemuel Patterson's life in Pittsburg, as the first of my ancestors to live here. His attempt at gold mining, his courtship of Ida White, his shoe store. And it was in her writing that I discovered a glimpse of Edward's childhood.

We said goodbye, and I shook Merton's hand. I wasn't sure when I'd see him again. I got into my rental car and drove away, headed for Krista's house. How many times had I traveled these roads since my father's death? I suspected I wouldn't be traveling them again soon—I could feel that this would be one of my last trips to Pittsburg for a while.

25.

No one was home when I arrived at Krista's. The door unlocked.

Her house is long and narrow, with a porch that wraps around the eastern side. I liked to imagine her fictional snake handlers gathering there after services, crating reptiles, drenched in sweat. Beyond the porch, the yard opened up to a small dead-end alley studded with willow and catalpa trees, and beyond that was Lakeside Park, a city park with a fishing lagoon. I let myself in and made my way to the bedroom on the main floor, where Krista had insisted I sleep. Across the room, on a dresser covered with framed photographs, I caught a glimpse of my mother in a portrait snapped in front of a sycamore tree. She's seated on the ground, her back against the bark. She wears a chambray denim shirt, a bandana in her hair, and an oversized silver ankh necklace. Her eyes are cast earthward and her right hand pulls at the grass, as if she's been caught in a drifting moment of modesty. Nearby was a picture of her sister, Rosemary, in a white crocheted hat. I walked over to the dresser and took other photographs from its surface, straining to identify each face.

I thought of the women in my family and the credit they deserve for surviving; they had tolerated the same lives the men had, lived through the grief of their deaths, and endured. I thought of Alta Faye, Leah, and my mother—all widows of suicide. Even if I didn't always understand their stoicism, I could see now their inner strength, their will to go on. Whatever I had inherited from the men in my family, I had inherited things from these women too. From Alta Faye, I inherited the powers of shrewd observation; from Leah, a calm disposition; and from my mother, a creative spirit. I went to sleep that night with all of them on my mind.

The next day I went to visit my grandmother Leah's house and found the sinkhole near the street.

When I think of the sinkhole today, I am gripped by a nauseating fear. I don't remember how long I stood peering at it, but once I reached my car, I belted myself in and sat in the driver's seat with the door closed, as if these things could make me safe. I could still see the huge depression and the house falling into it down the block, in the rearview mirror. I had never seen anything like it.

"I looked upon the scene before me—upon the mere house, and the simple landscape features of the domain," Edgar Allan Poe writes of such horror in "The Fall of the House of Usher." "Upon the bleak walls—upon the vacant eye-like windows—upon a few rank sedges—and upon a few white trunks of decayed trees—with an utter depression of soul which I can compare to no earthly sensation more properly than to the after-dream of the reveller upon opium—the bitter lapse into every-day life—the hideous dropping off of the veil."

I started the car and drove around town aimlessly. I followed Broadway to the south and entered the cemetery, but I didn't visit my father's grave. I just sat idling at the gate. I called Rachel, at home with our son, Finn. No answer. So I kept driving. I drove for miles past other small towns—Galena, Riverton, Baxter Springs—loosely tracing the route my maternal grandparents took when they eloped, until I reached Picher, Oklahoma, just south of the Kansas border. I'd read about Picher while researching the region's mining history, but I had never traveled across the county line. Now, as I edged into Ottawa County, I saw mountainous piles of chat, some more than two hundred feet high.

Picher—thirty miles south of Pittsburg—was "the 'buckle' of the mining belt that ran through Oklahoma, Kansas, and Missouri." The bonanza-rich mineral lodes of the Tri-State Mining District were first tapped around 1850. Within one hundred years, workers in Picher had extracted, processed, and sent out into the market most of the zinc and lead mined in the United States and produced more than $20 billion in ore.

Like Pittsburg, like all of America, Picher was founded through a bald acquisition of land. What would become Picher was once part of a Quapaw reservation. When lead and zinc were discovered, mining companies wanted to come in, but the Quapaw refused to lease their land. So the companies decided to acquire land through the Bureau of Indian Affairs (BIA) instead, having individual tribal members deemed incompetent. The BIA signed leases on those individuals' behalf, and Picher got its start as a twentieth-century boomtown.

In 1967, the mines shut down, although a strong sense of national and community pride lingered. "They ought to be putting a monument up there, out here, about the old miners [who] died here to get the lead out for the Army and Navy," Orval "Hoppy" Ray, who lived in Picher for eighty-four years, told the *Oklahoman*. Water contamination and extensive undermining had already taken their toll, however. In 1983, the town was declared a Superfund site by the EPA. By 2005, after a high number of Picher's children were found to have toxic levels of lead in their blood, the state started offering buyouts for residents to relocate. Then, on May 10, 2008, an EF4 tornado struck town. The twister flattened buildings, stripped trees, and destroyed more than a hundred houses. It was the last straw. The next year, the city ceased all operations. "All they want to do is shut the place down," Ray concluded in the town's waning years. "They don't care squat about anything around here."

Sites like this exist all over the country, some buried in plain sight. A 2001 *American Journal of Public Health* article revealed four hundred previously unknown lead smelters that operated before the creation of the EPA. In an effort to spur the government into action, William Eckel, an environmental scientist and the author of the study, paid to have soil tested in ten of the sites. All but one exceeded the EPA's hazard levels. More recent soil tests done by *USA TODAY* revealed twenty-one areas in thirteen states with potentially dangerous lead levels. The paper also reported systemic failures by government agencies to investigate dangers posed by the old sites, despite being alerted to the potential issues over a decade previous. The Superfund program has struggled financially and politically, and the EPA has lacked funds to complete even previously scheduled remediation projects, leaving a number of sites unaddressed. You can find maps online that reveal the risk of lead exposure across the country. In one, Pittsburg was rated ten out of ten for risk; the neighborhood in Minneapolis where I live now was rated nine.

Some of the old smelter sites in Crawford County are easily identified, yet—like Picher—remain unsafe wastelands. As part of Kansas's effort to test grounds surrounding former zinc smelters, the state's Department of Health and Environment (KDHE) identified nearly thirty smelter sites in southeastern Kansas. Many of these are orphan sites, meaning the parties responsible for the waste can't be found or "fail to act." The EPA's Superfund program is designed to clean up these sites, but the work is often coordinated through state and local agencies and requires state officials to not only conduct environmental investigations but also attempt to trace ownership. These investigations are expensive, which means the work of remediation can move at a glacial pace. And as removing soil from these sites is very costly, a more common—and cheaper—cleanup alternative is often used. Waste is consolidated and capped, the sites turned into streets and industrial lots. Pittsburg's Home Depot on North Broadway, for example, sits on the former site of the Weir City Zinc Company. Other sites, not yet remediated, remain in various stages of assessment and cleanup. A few are empty lots or fields with mounds of broken brick foundations still visible in the underbrush and acres of smelter waste; some are more conspicuous. At the former Eagle-Picher Mining and Smelting site in Galena, for example, a sixty-acre site remained filled with waste up to fifteen feet deep before remediation began in 2015. When reading accounts of these projects, I am struck by their air of casualness and pride. "The fifty years of zinc smelting in Kansas brought opportunity to thousands of workers and encouraged the development of new communities," a report from the KDHE reads. "The prosperity of the era also left behind a legacy of contaminated land that has resulted in millions of dollars of private and public funding to complete environmental cleanup."

A few miles outside of Picher, I pulled over to the side of the road and aimed my camera at the marked horizon. Trucks passed by, barreling down the highway. A few truckers pulled their horns as I snapped pictures of the chat piles that spread down the road, surrounded with barbed wire and government signs that warned against trespassing. What was left of Picher-Cardin High School sat in the shadows. I got back in the car, winding my way past the chat until I reached a fence blocking downtown.

When Picher was still alive, many of its fourteen thousand residents didn't see chat piles as sites of contamination. Children rode their bikes up and down them. Families climbed to the top for picnics. Some people filled their driveways with chat. Others used it in children's sandboxes, unaware of the poisoning taking place. Even for those who didn't come into close contact with the piles themselves, toxic dust was often carried on the wind. Surely that dust must also reach—or did once reach—Pittsburg. And surely, I was breathing lead into my lungs now. I closed my eyes and tried to imagine the scale of airborne pollution in the early days of industry. I could imagine the blackened skies over Pittsburg. I could imagine a vast amount of solid waste: the cinders from the coal-fired furnaces, the broken retorts, the impure burning slag blown away at the end of the smelting process.

How might these environmental conditions have affected my family? Depression? Anxiety? Suicide? And beyond these potential physical effects, what did it mean for my ancestors to have lived in this industrial sacrifice zone?

"Sacrifice is a historically and culturally ubiquitous, yet disunified and shape-shifting practice," political scientist Wendy Brown reminds us in *Undoing the Demos: Neoliberalism's Stealth Revolution.* "It has supremely religious, as well as utterly prosaic usages—there are ritual sacrifices of animals and other treasures to god(s), parental sacrifices of time, sleep, and money for children, and strategic sacrifices in games—of a pawn in chess or to advance a runner in baseball. . . . Sacrifice is a communal ritual that renarrates the community's origin and expresses its conscious dependence on the sacred, but is distinct from other expressions of devotion or servitude in that we feed the life-giving powers of the sacred with life."

I parked my car and squeezed under the fence. I walked only as far as one city block into the town's center. Around the perimeter, slabs of concrete and brick foundations stood in neat rows where there were once houses; sidewalks, eroded and fractured, were littered with bluestem and clover; driveways ended abruptly. Up and down the street, storefronts were boarded up. A parking lot had been turned into a dumping ground filled with tires, the charred remains of a mattress tossed in the road. I walked in and out of a few houses. Some were entirely empty. Some contained objects carefully arranged: pictures of Jesus, a teddy bear propped in a kitchen sink, a clock on the threshold of an open door. Could that be what it looks like when it all ends? To know facts and figures surrounding any environmental degradation is one thing, but to witness the destruction, or its aftermath, is another. I didn't feel horror so much as fascination as I panned through the landscape with the camera's lens. I had entered the harsh particulars of a sacrifice zone, where life had been offered not to the sacred but to the capitalist instinct. Most of the trees and grass were dead, and yet the abandoned mill sites held a beautiful if unsettling kind of wilderness; blooming vines and roses trailed over the old foundations and the rubbish skeletons of houses, purple martins nesting in their eaves. In 2015, more than a thousand migratory birds would be found dead here, killed by a suspected zinc poisoning.

As martins circled above, I walked toward a junk heap of televisions, mattresses, and random appliances, only to realize that it was actually a sinkhole filled with trash. This was appropriate; for many years, sinkholes have been used as trash dumps. But in the Mayan civilization, sinkholes were thought of as sacred entries to the afterlife, with precious objects tossed down as a ritual to assuage further passage.

"In the language of geologists," writes journalist Jon Henley in the *Guardian*, the process that causes sinkholes "is 'the creation of a void which migrates towards the surface.'"

In the language of prophets: a biblical sign of judgment, rapture, a trumpet sound, a celestial metaphor for the end of days. "Now it came to pass, as he finished speaking all these words, that the ground split apart under them, and the earth opened its mouth and swallowed them."

I saw only one sink that day in Picher, but later learned the town was riddled with them. After the town was deemed unlivable because of lead toxicity, the Army Corps of Engineers also "confirmed that more than a third of the homes . . . were undermined by massive voids." Picher was "in danger of catastrophic subsidence." A 2006 report detailing sinkhole threats in the town makes it clear that one day a number of open shafts will inevitably give way and leave Picher swallowed in earth.

That afternoon, I went back to Pittsburg and to the sink near my grandmother's house. It was no longer as quiet as it had been that morning. Trucks full of cement and gravel idled in the street. Men stood nearby in neon safety vests and hard hats, with shovels in their hands. And a few of the neighbors had finally emerged from their houses, setting up lawn chairs in the street as though observing a parade. One man had a cooler; another sat under a shade umbrella, which he pushed into the boulevard grass.

Despite all the activity, the sinkhole wasn't huge news. When I looked in the *Pittsburg Morning Sun* to read about it, I found only one item, buried on page three. The hole had appeared just a few days before, a Wednesday: "It all started with a knock."

"I was having my tea and reading the *Morning Sun* when I heard what sounded like a knock on the side of the house," Gloria Oertle, the home's owner, said in the newspaper account. "A few minutes passed, and it did it again. The third time it happened, it sounded like a bird hit the window or something. That's when I went outside."

When Gloria walked out onto the lawn, she was surprised to see that one corner of her house had dropped two inches into the ground. Back inside the house, enormous cracks began to appear in the walls as she went to the phone to call for help. Crews immediately arrived on the scene. Men drilled holes in the ground around the perimeter of the sink and filled them with cement, attempting to stop the ground from shifting. But the hole kept growing. And the house kept slipping, the foundation ripping away, collapsing slowly into the sink. A few days passed: workers remained to make sure the house didn't disappear into the hole, while engineers figured out what to do next. Eventually, workers pulled the house from its foundation, placed it on beams and cribbing, and pushed it to the edge of the yard—the way I would see it—for many months.

Years later, I interviewed Larry Spahn, an environmental technician with the state's surface mining section, about Gloria Oertle's yard. *We named that operation the big dig*, he told me. *It was a pretty big hole, but not as bad as the one we handled in Galena:* the sink I mentioned earlier, the one that swallowed the two-story apartment building in 2006.

Back then, Spahn described the prevalence of sinkholes in the area to the *Joplin Globe* as "an ongoing problem that's left over from the area's mining legacy. A lot of money came out of the ore and coalfields. Now we're reaping the problems. I don't think mine owners had any regard for where they were digging. They didn't have the regulations in place that we have today. The mine owners were gods, more or less."

In the evening, I called Rachel again. It had been a sleepless night for her and Finn, and she sounded exhausted. When she asked how I was, I ignored my careless drive across the border and instead told her about the sinkhole. I tried to give her enough detail to create a precise picture, one that might convey the enormity of the image, but with each attempt, I felt myself struggling.

As I stood in the yard outside my cousin's house, grasping for words, I could hear Finn, now almost two, in the background. I felt a yearning inside, an odd mixture of elation and misgiving.

—*I'm sorry*, I said.

—*For what?* she asked.

—*For being away right now.*

—*It's okay, as long as you're coming back.*

Sweat stained the collar of my T-shirt. My arms hung heavy and my feet throbbed. Trees in a nearby park lurched in the wind. My mind faltered over memories of loose rock careening out of the dump truck's bed; of the house cribbed on steel planks; of plowed fields and spoil banks; of the remediated wilderness of southeastern Kansas; of pit lakes, green in summer's radiance; of the sycamore, now fallen, that had wavered above my father's grave; of railroad beds trailing the highway; of ancestral deathscapes; of gravel roads and bluestem prairie, hickory and cherry trees, sandstone and limestone and clay.

It traveled past streams, rivers, and bridges, to the sharp angled roof of our house, the rim of a large window's gloss; to the living room, and to the flat surface of our bookshelf, strewn with rocks, sticks, and a stack of books waiting to be read. Here, talking with Rachel, I felt the need to close the door on Pittsburg, to end my obsessive search for answers.

Across the alley, in the park, I could see a glimmer of water through the trees. Slowly, a flickering insight arrived: the search I'd undertaken—set off by a death, set off by a trail of things left by my father—had helped me not only to feel my grief but to transform the pain of it. I can remember this moment with particular vividness. As Rachel and I sat on the phone quietly—but not, I reflected, listening to those faints sounds from Finn, silently—I thought about all the darkness I'd faced over the past three years. I had spent so much time considering what had been taken from me, but for the first time, I felt that its lasting effects might be a deeper trust in all that I had been given.

26.

Before Finn was born, I spent an evening with a friend visiting from out of town. When I picked Joseph up at his hotel, he was wearing his familiar black Blundstone boots, khaki pants, a button-down shirt, and vintage eyeglasses. We hadn't seen each other in a while, and a lot of rough things had happened; it was close to the one-year anniversary of my father's death and one month after my release from the hospital. Our night together was long. We went to a dimly lit bar near the Mississippi River. That night the place was pretty empty, so we sidled up to the large mirrored bar at the back of the room, near the kitchen. He coaxed me into ordering a whiskey straight, like my paternal grandfather would. *Consider it research*, he said. Once I told him about my car accident and the events surrounding my father's death, once I'd enumerated my questions about my father's suicide and suicide in general, once we'd pondered the historical past and the future, then we talked (as we often did) about poetry and the impending climate crisis the world faced. After I confessed that the unprecedented heat haunted me, we reached the question of parenthood: he wanted to know if I'd come to terms with the idea. I rattled off my list of fears and reservations as we ordered another drink. Joseph had two children of his own, and over the years we had talked openly and frankly about the intricacies of parenthood. At the end of the evening, when I dropped him off at his hotel, he got out of the car and then leaned through the open passenger door.

—*You're a poet. So maybe you just need the language to guide you,* he said. *Think less about parenting, more about stewarding a soul.*

Stewarding a soul: I thought of Keats's "Call the world if you please, 'The vale of Soul-making,'" a line I've always loved. Joseph flashed a grin and shut the door. And as I watched him turn and walk into the hotel lobby, I felt for a moment the precision of his advice. The word *soul* is delicate. As a writer, I often avoid using it. But Joseph knew me well, and he knew that I needed to reshape my state of mind. Grief and parenthood had become intertwined for me: the future was frightening. But time wouldn't stop for me. I needed to figure out not just how to exist within it, but how to embrace it.

Finn is eleven now. He's been alive almost as long as I've been writing this book. I have been slow. Sometimes stalled or blocked. Parenting—and its emotional demands—have often asked me to set writing aside. But, in writing's absence, I've also learned to be more present.

My mother still lives in the house my parents purchased when I was born, the house my father slipped out of in the middle of that December night more than ten years ago. How many Tuesdays have turned to Wednesdays since then? As I write this, I've lost the thread of counting, the thread of time. I also realize that I really have no idea how to bring this story—his story, their story, our story—to an end, other than to reveal this present moment, which has already slipped away. Later, it will rain, and I'll call my mother to check in on her, as I often do. She and I seldom talk about my father, and it's at least partly my fault. I used to make a point of acknowledging his birthday and the anniversary of his death, but over time the habit has slipped. Maybe it's fine. Maybe it's okay to let some rituals go. Maybe this is just what it means to come from a long line of women who are vanquishers, survivors. We've each had to make our own way through trauma and grief. We've each had to decide what to keep and what to let go.

I've slowly replaced the ad hoc display of ancestral research in the room where I write with Finn's drawings—some framed, others simply taped to the wall. Little by little, one kind of map has replaced another: what once was the blueprint of an investigation is now an assembly of devotion. The historical photos of Pittsburg were the first to go, replaced by a cartoon rendering of a duck. Next went the portraits of my father and of Edward, and in came a different kind of picture, of a pink and blue colored-marker bird perched on a wire, with a large teardrop falling from its eye. From the bird's beak, a speech bubble hovers in a nickel-gray sky: *I am a sad bird.* Then a collection of pencil drawings that Finn presented from his backpack, folded in neat squares, took the place of other artifacts. Now the wall displays a thunder of dragons, a sketch of an apartment building in the rain, and an early family portrait. In the drawing, three stick figures, holding tiny hands, stand encased in a heart.

Finn already knows about the men who are lost—dead—to my family. He knows about suicide. I haven't hidden that from him. Nor have I hidden my father. I make a point to talk about him when I can, and sometimes I catch myself repeating some of the things he taught me when I was a kid—how to grip a tennis racket, snap a Frisbee, or pull out a nail with a hammer claw. And, in faithfulness to a child's curiosity, I've had to see some things anew: bulldozers, bridges, knot tying and the history of particular breeds of dogs. I've had to learn to tell stories—not fictional stories (though we do that too), but true stories that unfold backward and forward in time.

My search for my family's history has ended, but the story still evolves. There's still grieving to do as we careen toward ecological disasters, as I see the mistakes of Pittsburg writ large on a global scale. As I see a devastating legacy of another kind coming for my son and, one day, his children. But I am grateful, nevertheless, to still be alive. And as a parent, I've been reshaped by a deep allegiance to the future, which changes my view of life itself. Whatever I've missed, I understand this now. I know I've got to keep moving ahead, with all my sorrows and doubts. And I can live with that.

Notes

"transient tempest in the mind" Edwin S. Shneidman, "Suicide as Psychache," in *Lives and Deaths: Selections from the Works of Edwin S. Shneidman*, ed. Antoon A. Leenaars (Philadelphia: Taylor & Francis, 1999), 242.

"I am working out" Muriel Rukeyser, "The Speed of Darkness," in *Out of Silence: Selected Poems* (Evanston, IL: TriQuarterly Books, 1992), 135.

"And the end of all our exploring" T. S. Eliot, "Little Gidding," in *Four Quartets* (New York: Harcourt Brace & Company, 1943), 59.

8   *in Greek superstition* Encyclopedia Britannica Online, s.v. "Number Symbolism," by Ian Stewart, accessed November 24, 2021, https://www.britannica.com/topic/number-symbolism.

9   *A haiku was often written* Harold G. Henderson, William J. Higginson, and Anita Virgil, "Definitions of Haiku and Related Terms: Previous 1973 Definitions," Haiku Society of America, accessed November 24, 2021, https://www.hsa-haiku.org/hsa-definitions.html#Defs1973.

9   *Seventeen is an ominous number* Nick Harris, "Bad Omen for Italy as Their Unlucky Number Comes Up," *Independent* (UK), November 15, 2007, https://www.independent.co.uk/sport/football/european/bad-omen-for-italy-as-their-unlucky-number-comes-up-400380.html.

12   *we stood guard* Rainer Maria Rilke to Paula Modersohn-
Becker, Bremen, February 12, 1902, in *Letters of Rainer Maria
Rilke: 1892–1910*, trans. Jane Bannard Greene and M. D.
Herter Norton (New York: W. W. Norton, 1969), 65.

15   *About forty of them* John A. Weeks III, "Bridges and
Structures of the Major Rivers of Minneapolis and Saint
Paul," personal website, accessed November 22, 2021, http://
johnweeks.com/bridges/index.html.

15   *Bridge #62075* "Historic Bridges," Minnesota Department of
Transportation, accessed February 9, 2009, https://www.dot.
state.mn.us/historicbridges/62075.html.

15   *Trees are more common* Olive Bennewith et al., "Suicide
by Hanging: Multicentre Study Based on Coroners' Records
in England," *British Journal of Psychiatry* 186, no. 3 (March
2005): 260.

16   *And why hanging* Lucy Biddle et al., "Factors Influencing
the Decision to Use Hanging as a Method of Suicide:
Qualitative Study," *British Journal of Psychiatry* 197, no. 4
(October 2010): 320.

20   *robins were appearing* Elizabeth Kolbert, *Field Notes from
a Catastrophe: Man, Nature, and Climate Change* (New York:
Bloomsbury, 2006), 64.

20   *Baby robins typically* Laura Erickson, "Baby Robins,"
Journey North, accessed November 22, 2021, https://
journeynorth.org/tm/robin/facts_baby_robins.html.

24   *According to psychologist Thomas Joiner* Thomas Joiner,
Myths about Suicide (Cambridge, MA: Harvard University
Press, 2011), 74.

24 *"differentiat[ing] explanations"* This quote, as well as the
summary of the work of other psychologists that precedes
it, comes from E. David Klonsky and Alexis M. May, "The
Three-Step Theory (3ST): A New Theory of Suicide Rooted
in the 'Ideation to Action' Framework," *International Journal of
Cognitive Therapy* 8, no. 2 (June 2015): 115.

25 *a new framework to address this query* Thomas Joiner
et al., "Main Predictions of the Interpersonal-Psychological
Theory of Suicidal Behavior: Empirical Tests in Two Samples
of Young Adults," *Journal of Abnormal Psychology* 118, no. 3
(August 2009): 2.

25 *"A nagging fact"* Thomas Joiner, *Why People Die by Suicide*
(Cambridge, MA: Harvard University Press, 2007), 1.

25 *"exact some revenge for it"* Thomas Joiner, interview by
Phil McGraw, *Dr. Phil Show,* January 2, 2009, 0:48, https://
www.youtube.com/watch?v=Jrjf3V7Tc1c.

26 **Psychiatrists Terry Martin and Kenneth Doka** Terry L.
Martin and Kenneth J. Doka, *Men Don't Cry . . . Women Do:
Transcending Gender Stereotypes of Grief* (Philadelphia: Brunner/
Mazel, 2000), 2.

46 **The stock market crash of September 2008** "Crash
Course," *Economist*, September 7, 2013, https://www.
economist.com/schools-brief/2013/09/07/crash-course.

47 *8.7 million jobs* Stephanie Hugie Barello, "Consumer
Spending and U.S. Employment from the 2007–2009
Recession through 2022," *Monthly Labor Review*, US Bureau of
Labor Statistics, October 2014, https://www.bls.gov/opub/
mlr/2014/article/consumer-spending-and-us-employment-
from-the-recession-through-2022.htm.

47   **more than ten thousand suicides** Aaron Reeves, Martin McKee, and David Stuckler, "Economic Suicides in the Great Recession in Europe and North America," *British Journal of Psychiatry* 205, no. 3 (September 2014): 246.

55   **"one of the finest characters"** 86 Cong. Rec. 1378 (1940).

55   **"honestly and sincerely"** Edward White Patterson, *Shall Our Government Go Forward or Backward?* (pamphlet), Congressional Papers of E. W. Patterson, Wichita State University Libraries Special Collections, Wichita, KS.

58   **"When the body was found"** "E. W. Patterson Shot to Death," *Baxter Springs (KS) Citizen*, March 11, 1940.

58   **it was hardly legible** "Suicide Note Left: Patterson Apparently Shot Self," *Columbus (KS) Daily Advocate*, March 8, 1940.

58   **"I must ask you to excuse me"** "Suicide Note Left," *Columbus (KS) Daily Advocate*.

59   **the gift of my grandmother** There is some ambiguity here. Wichita State University's website credits Dan Carney, a prominent Wichita businessman and a cofounder of Pizza Hut, with donating these materials. But my uncle Merton told me that Leah had collected the materials and made the arrangements for donation, and indeed the boxes at the library were marked with her name. The librarian I spoke with could not explain the discrepancy.

59   **"most personal papers"** Center of Legislative Archives, "Congressional Collections," National Archives, accessed March 2022, https://www.archives.gov/legislative/repository-collections.

63   *It was a flourishing wilderness* Home Authors, *A Twentieth Century History and Biographical Record of Crawford County, Kansas* (Chicago: Lewis Publishing Company, 1905), 7.

63   *"when the sun disappeared"* History and Biographical Record of Crawford County, 7.

63   *"It was a goodly land"* Nathaniel Thompson Allison, *History of Cherokee County, Kansas and Representative Citizens* (Chicago: Biographical Publishing Company, University of Chicago, 1904), 23.

72   *"Red-headed, fearless and full of fight"* This and the following quote are from contemporary newspapers I read in my grandfather's archive, but I was unable to confirm the sources at a later date.

72   *"callous disregard for the unemployed"* Patterson, *Shall Our Government Go Forward or Backward?*

72   *The 1930 Federal Unemployment Census* Peter Fearon, *Kansas in the Great Depression: Work Relief, the Dole, and Rehabilitation* (Columbia, MO: University of Missouri Press, 2007), 15.

72   *By November 1931* Fearon, 25.

73   *"children were wrapped"* Fearon, 33.

73   *"The liquor traffic"* Fearon, 33.

74   *"economic security of the people"* Edward White Patterson, "Radio Address on the General Welfare Act," September 25, 1938, KOAM Radio, Pittsburg, KS.

74   *"restored the banking system"* Louis Menand, "How the Deal Went Down," *New Yorker*, March 4, 2013,

https://www.newyorker.com/magazine/2013/03/04/
how-the-deal-went-down.

74   *the New Deal was made possible* To understand the
New Deal and the role of the Southern Democrats, I relied
on Menand, "How the Deal Went Down"; Willow Lung-
Amam, "The Next New Deal Must Be for Black Americans,
Too," Bloomberg CityLab, January 18, 2021, https://www.
bloomberg.com/news/articles/2021-01-18/the-next-new-deal-
must-be-for-black-americans-too; and Jefferson Cowie and
Nick Salvatore, "The Long Exception: Rethinking the Place
of the New Deal in American History," *International Labor and
Working-Class History* 74, no. 74 (Fall 2008).

75   *"exercised strict control"* Menand, "How the Deal Went
Down."

75   *"human rights"* Edward White Patterson, campaign card,
1938, Congressional Papers of E. W. Patterson, Wichita State
University Libraries Special Collections, Wichita, KS.

77   *March 6, 1940, a Wednesday* To imagine the fictional scenes
describing Edward's death, I referenced a number of historical
sources to identify specific locations and buildings in Pittsburg
during that period. Newspaper articles and my father's own
personal notes (which he partially derived from an interview
with his sister) helped me to imagine a timeline of events
associated with his death and the events that immediately
followed. Finally, I approximated the drive Edward might have
taken that day, culminating with the site where he died.

85   *Naylor Funeral Home in Weir* At least two newspaper
accounts cite the Naylor chapel or Naylor-Quinn Mortuary
(in Pittsburg) as the location where the body was taken. But

the account detailing the coroner's inquest suggests the body was held at the Naylor-Quinn chapel in Weir, once named the Naylor Funeral Home.

85 *"outstanding evidence of suicide"* "Suicide Note Left," *Columbus (KS) Daily Advocate.*

85 *the inquest convened* "Death Inquest Continued: No Surprising Development in Patterson Inquest at Weir," *Modern Light* (Columbus, KS), March 21, 1940.

86 *"on a lonely road"* "Death Inquest Continued," *Modern Light* (Columbus, KS).

86 *My grandfather was buried* Like the rest of my re-creation of Edward's death, this scene of his funeral draws on a combination of contemporary newspaper sources and my own imagination.

90 *"There are indications of suicide"* "Patterson Funeral to Be Held Tomorrow," *Columbus (KS) Daily Advocate,* March 8, 1940.

92 *"no information was brought out"* "Death Inquest Continued," *Modern Light* (Columbus, KS).

92 *"county attorney had said"* "Death Inquest Continued," *Modern Light* (Columbus, KS).

93 *Pittsburg's chapter boasted* Lila Lee Jones, "The Ku Klux Klan in Eastern Kansas during the 1920s," *Emporia State Research Studies* 23, no. 3 (Winter 1975): 5.

93 *several sundown towns* "Alphabetical Map of Sundown Towns by State," History & Social Justice, Tougaloo College, accessed December 15, 2021, https://justice.tougaloo.edu/sundown-towns/using-the-sundown-towns-database/state-map/.

93 *"drew white Protestants"* Kathleen Belew, *Bring the War Home: The White Power Movement and Paramilitary America* (Cambridge, MA: Harvard University Press, 2018), 36.

93 *"Preachers often welcomed"* James N. Leiker, "The Klan in the Coal Mines: The End of Kansas's Reform Era in the 1920s," *Western Historical Quarterly* 48, no. 3 (Autumn 2017): 286.

93 *"crime and anarchy"* Leiker, 287.

94 *"lawless spirit"* Patrick G. O'Brien, Kenneth J. Peak, and Barbara K. Robins, "'It May Have Been Illegal, but It Wasn't Wrong': The Kansas 'Balkans' Bootlegging Culture, 1920–1940," *Kansas History: A Journal of the Central Plains* 11, no. 4 (Winter 1988–1989): 262.

94 *"over-run with the worst cut throats"* Eugene DeGruson, "The European Influence and Experience: Ethnicity and Southeast Kansas" (unpublished paper, Special Collections, Leonard H. Axe Library, Pittsburg State University, 1991), quoted in Leiker, "Klan in the Coal Mines," 280.

94 *an outdoors Klan meeting* Jones, "Ku Klux Klan in Eastern Kansas," 18.

94 *they endorsed A. H. Carl* Jones, 18.

94 *a campaign of eliminating bootlegging* O'Brien, Peak, and Robins, "It May Have Been Illegal," 270.

95 *"active chapter of the Black Hand"* Leiker, "Klan in the Coal Mines," 280.

95 *"predecessor of the mafia"* Leiker, 280.

95   *"loud, gravelly voice"* J. T. Knoll, "Saia's Chicken Yard," *Pittsburg Morning Sun*, September 14, 2014.

95   *He believed, according to one interview* Steven Baden, "D. J. 'Joe' Saia: The Padrone of Crawford County" (master's thesis, Kansas State College of Pittsburg, 1975), https://digitalcommons.pittstate.edu/etd/133.

95   *Edward appointed Saia relief supervisor* J. T. Knoll, "Joe Saia—Labor Leader and Union Man," *Pittsburg Morning Sun*, September 14, 2014.

96   *"I am bitterly opposed"* Knoll, "Joe Saia—Labor Leader."

96   *"extorted money from its victims"* O'Brien, Peak, and Robins, "It May Have Been Illegal," 262.

96   *"violent acts were committed"* O'Brien, Peak, and Robins, 262.

97   *"local tough guys"* J. T. Knoll, in discussion with the author, October 2021.

97   *Frontenac, the bootlegging hub* Most local historians agree on the presence of bootlegging and of criminality in Frontenac, but not all claim ties to organized crime. My references here include Patrick G. O'Brien and Kenneth J. Peak, *Kansas Bootleggers* (Topeka: Sunflower University Press, 1991); Dean Sims, *Hard Rock: Historical Fiction of a Boy Growing Up amid Tragedy in the World's Largest Lead and Zinc Mining Field* (New York: Writers Club Press, 2003); and Jerry Lomshek, in discussion with the author in Chicopee, KS, July 2012.

97   *"all fantasyland"* J. T. Knoll, in discussion with the author, October 2021.

97   *"master politician"* Knoll, discussion.

97   *"rough and tumble guy"* Knoll, discussion.

101   *"We have now been at work"* "Diary of William L.
      Patterson of His Trip to the Black Hills of Dakota in
      the Year 1877," transcribed in Belle White Rush, "Your
      Heritage through Your Grandmother Ida White Patterson"
      (unpublished manuscript, 1958).

101   *"make some mush"* "Diary of William L. Patterson," in
      Rush, "Your Heritage."

101   *"some Pilgrims"* "Diary of William L. Patterson," in Rush,
      "Your Heritage."

101   *"We have made arrangements"* "Diary of William L.
      Patterson," in Rush, "Your Heritage."

102   *"Pittsburg, for miles around"* Prosperous Pittsburg, Pictorially
      Portrayed (Pittsburg, KS: Pittsburg Publicity Company, 1915),
      accessed via "Pittsburg Scenes—Mining," Pittsburg Kansas—
      Memories, http://pittsburgksmemories.com/Pittsburg_
      Mining/pittmining2.html.

103   *Pittsburg was founded in 1876* For historical background
      about Pittsburg's mining industry, I relied on these sources:
      M. Augustine Clarahan, "The Founding and Early
      Development of Pittsburg" (master's thesis, Kansas State
      Teachers College, 1934), https://digitalcommons.pittstate.
      edu/etd/110; Fred N. Howell, "Some Phases of the Industrial
      History of Pittsburg, Kansas," *Kansas Historical Quarterly*
      1, no. 3 (May 1932); Frank Layden, "A Study of Some of
      the Problems of Settlement of Crawford County, Kansas"
      (master's thesis, Kansas State Teachers College, 1938), https://

digitalcommons.pittstate.edu/etd/145; and John Skubitz Jr., "A History of the Development of Deep Mine Production in Crawford County and the Factors That Have Influenced It" (master's thesis, Kansas State Teachers College, 1934), https:// digitalcommons.pittstate.edu/etd/149.

103 *a British-born entrepreneur named Robert Lanyon* History and Biographical Record of Crawford County, 107.

103 *"Smelters ran 24 hours a day"* Aspen Junge and Rick Bean, *A Short History of the Zinc Smelting Industry in Kansas* (Topeka: Bureau of Environmental Remediation, Kansas Department of Health and Environment, 2006), 4.

103 *It was a dirty, dangerous business* Information about the hazards involved in smelting I gleaned largely from Junge and Bean, *A Short History of the Zinc Smelting Industry in Kansas.*

104 *As the Kansas coal mines expanded* William E. Powell, "Europeans Attracted by Mines," *Alumnian: A Journal for Graduates of Kansas State Teachers College* (Spring 1976): 4–8.

104 *labor disputes between 1882 and 1895* Ann Schofield, "An 'Army of Amazons': The Language of Protest in a Kansas Mining Community, 1921–22," *American Quarterly* 37, no. 5 (Winter 1985): 691.

104 *12 percent of the workforce* Leiker, "Klan in the Coal Mines," 280.

104 *agents met immigrants* Schofield, "Army of Amazons," 691.

104 *"paradise on Earth"* Olive L. Sullivan, "Amazon Army Raid on Coal Mines Remembered at Chicopee Lecture," *Pittsburg Morning Sun*, March 26, 2001.

104 *"a polyglot area peopled"* Schofield, "Army of Amazons," 691.

105 *"Coal soot has blackened"* May Wood Simons, "Mining Coal and Maiming Men," *Coming Nation* (Girard, KS), November 11, 1911, quoted in Powell, "Europeans Attracted by Mines," 8.

105 *"cave-ins, falling rock, explosions"* Matt DeMoss, "A Missed Opportunity: The Failure to Unionize Little Balkan Miners during the Strikes of 1893" (undergraduate research, Pittsburg State University, 2009), 3, https://digitalcommons. pittstate.edu/hist/4.

105 *Workers were paid* Information about life in the mining camps comes from these sources: Leiker, "Klan in the Coal Mines"; DeMoss, "Missed Opportunity"; and Powell, "Europeans Attracted by Mines."

106 *"I might as well be governor"* Walter Stubbs, quoted in Leiker, "Klan in the Coal Mines," 280.

106 *"pay homage to the region's history"* "Little Balkans Days," Little Balkans Festival, accessed March 17, 2019, https://littlebalkansfestival.com/.

106 *The Little Balkans were also politically distinct* Schofield, "Army of Amazons," 693.

106 *made Girard his home* Schofield, 693.

106 *"Socialist intellectuals seemed to understand"* Leiker, "Klan in the Coal Mines," 282.

107 *"the war made such successes"* Leiker, 283.

107 *"Bull of the Woods"* "The Passing of Mr. Howat," *Labor Digest* 16, no. 2 (February 1924): 13.

107 ***Christened the "Amazon Army"*** For a more detailed
history of these events, I recommend: Benjamin W. Goosen,
"'Like a Brilliant Thread': Gender and Vigilante Democracy
in the Kansas Coalfield, 1921–1922," *Kansas History: A Journal
of the Central Plains* 34, no. 3 (Autumn 2011); and Schofield,
"Army of Amazons."

108 ***"if, instead of going on the run"*** Rush, "Your Heritage."

113 ***a sinkhole is sometimes called a snake hole*** Daniel
F. Merriam and C. John Mann, "Sinkholes and Related
Geologic Features in Kansas," *Transactions of the Kansas Academy
of Science* 60, no. 3 (Fall 1957).

113 ***In 2005, federal agencies*** Sheila K. Stogsdill, "Sinkhole
Search Begins for Missing Welch Girls," *Oklahoman,* June
29, 2005, https://www.oklahoman.com/article/2902081/
sinkhole-search-begins-for-missing-welch-girls-br-underwater-
camera-used-in-flooded-kansas-pit.

114 ***Sinkholes have plagued southeastern Kansas*** Daniel
F. Merriam, "Surface Sinkholes and Other Solution
Features," in *Geologic History of Kansas* (Lawrence: Kansas
State Geological Survey, University of Kansas, 1963),
accessed May 2012, https://www.kgs.ku.edu/Publications/
Bulletins/162/10_app_d.html.

114 ***the hole that opened up*** Mike Belt, "Mining's Legacy:
A Scar on Kansas," *Lawrence Journal-World*, March 20,
2007, https://www2.ljworld.com/news/2007/mar/20/
minings_legacy_scar_kansas/.

114 ***In 2006, a two-story apartment building*** Belt, "Mining's
Legacy."

114   *The* **World Property Journal** Francys Vallecillo, "2013: Year of the Sinkhole in U.S.," *World Property Journal*, December 11, 2013, https://www.worldpropertyjournal.com/north-america-residential-news/2013-us-natural-disasters-natural-hazard-risk-for-us-corelogic-7754.php.

114   *a man named Jeff Bush* Rick Jervis, "Body Buried in Fla. Sinkhole Leaves Troubling Questions," *USA Today*, March 16, 2013, https://www.usatoday.com/story/news/nation/2013/03/16/body-sinkhole-buried/1987861/.

114   *Pennsylvania sinkholes* John Ostapkovich, "Pennsylvania Boasts Large Number of Sinkholes," 3 CBS Philly, March 11, 2013, https://philadelphia.cbslocal.com/2013/03/11/pennsylvania-boasts-large-number-of-sinkholes/.

114   *a sinkhole in the Westmoreland neighborhood* "Drone Goes Inside a 100 Feet Wide Sinkhole in Gainesville Neighborhood," WCJB-TV 20, November 11, 2020, https://www.wcjb.com/2020/11/12/watch-drone-goes-inside-a-100-feet-wide-sinkhole-in-gainesville-neighborhood/.

115   *I watched footage* Tim Murphy, "Meet the Town That's Being Swallowed by a Sinkhole," *Mother Jones*, August 2013, https://www.motherjones.com/environment/2013/08/bayou-corne-sinkhole-disaster-louisiana-texas-brine/. Video accompanied the story: https://www.motherjones.com/politics/2013/08/watch-bayou-corne-sinkhole-swallow-forest/.

116   *Cherokee County, most of Crawford County* Allison, *History of Cherokee County.*

117   *a growing white population* History and Biographical Record of Crawford County, 3–5.

117 *"the most extensive, radical, redistributive"* Keri
Leigh Merritt, "Land and the Roots of African-American
Poverty," *Aeon*, March 11, 2016, https://aeon.co/ideas/
land-and-the-roots-of-african-american-poverty.

122 *"more than 1,500 open shafts"* "Cleanup from Mining in
Kansas," Kansas Geological Survey, University of Kansas,
accessed December 2021, https://geokansas.ku.edu/
cleanup-from-mining-kansas.

122 *"including 599 mine hazards"* "Cleanup from Mining in
Kansas."

122 *"Hell's Half-Acre"* Roger McKinney, "Unsteady Ground,"
Joplin (KS) Globe, September 24, 2006, https://www.
joplinglobe.com/news/local_news/unsteady-ground/
article_7576a5bf-f491-5d2f-a98c-786bb2ca1b23.html.

122 *Spencer Chemical planted the ridges* Howell, "Industrial
History of Pittsburg."

122 *Pittsburg citizens bought* Howell, "Industrial History of
Pittsburg."

127 *According to varying historical accounts* To
understand Yale's history as a mining camp, I consulted the
following sources: Home Authors, *A Twentieth Century History
and Biographical Record of Crawford County, Kansas*; Index of
Names, Crawford County, United States Federal Census
1900, accessed via Ancestry.com; and "Other Towns &
Coal Camps of Crawford County, Kansas," Pittsburg,
Kansas—Memories, accessed March 2012, http://www.
pittsburgksmemories.com/Crawford_County/CC_Towns/
cctownothers.html.

128 *"members of the black community"* John M. Robb, *The Black Coal Miner of Southeast Kansas* (Topeka: State of Kansas Commission on Civil Rights, 1969), 4–5.

128 *trains departed Birmingham* Robb, *Black Coal Miner*, 5.

128 *flanked by US Marshals* Chase Rietcheck, "The Major Strike in Pittsburg, Kansas: Strike of 1899 on the Major Coal Mining Strike of 1899" (undergraduate research, Pittsburg State University, 2009), 10, https:// digitalcommons.pittstate.edu/hist/5.

128 *The strike ended* Rietcheck, "Major Strike," 13.

132 *The pottery opened in 1888* "Biographical Note," Pittsburg Pottery Company Collection, 1983–94, Special Collections, Leonard H. Axe Library, Pittsburg State University, https://digitalcommons.pittstate.edu/ fa/266; and "Pittsburg Pottery Company," Pittsburg, Kansas—Memories, accessed April 20, 2013, http:// www.pittsburgksmemories.com/Pittsburg_Buildings/ pittbldgpittburgpottery.html.

132 *The company began producing flowerpots* J. T. Knoll, "True Stories: Pittsburg Pottery Molded More Than Stoneware," *Pittsburg Morning Sun*, February 28, 2010.

132 *the plant's employees organized* My mother and my cousin Krista verify this story; however, I was unable to locate a source to confirm these facts. It's possible or even likely that the "strike" was not reported on, as it may have been neither an official union strike nor a prolonged event.

133 *the pottery took orders* Knoll, "Pittsburg Pottery."

134   *it was purchased by Gulf Oil* Richard Rutter, "Gulf Oil Seeking Fertilizer Maker," *New York Times*, September 11, 1963.

134   *Gulf's growth rate during the 1950s* "About Gulf," Gulf Oil, accessed via Wayback Machine on November 24, 2021, https://www.gulfoil.com/history3.html.

136   *The immediate cause of death* This information comes from my grandfather's certificate of death, dated October 30, 1967.

149   *"Mr. McCluskey was said"* "Body Located in Strip Pit near Cherokee," *Pittsburg Headlight*, September 28, 1967.

149   *a monoamine oxidase inhibitor* Francisco López-Muñoz et al., "Half a Century of Antidepressant Drugs: On the Clinical Introduction of Monoamine Oxidase Inhibitors, Tricyclics, and Tetracyclics," *Journal of Clinical Psychopharmacology* 27, no. 6 (December 2007).

149   *including, on rare occasions, anxiety* "Monoamine Oxidase Inhibitors (MAOIS)," Mayo Clinic, https://www.mayoclinic.org/diseases-conditions/depression/in-depth/maois/art-20043992.

156   *only about 15 to 25 percent* Joiner, *Myths about Suicide*, 119.

156   *"Most decedents feel alienated"* Thomas Joiner, "Understanding and Overcoming the Myths of Suicide," *Psychiatric Times* 28, no. 1 (January 2011).

156   *"one working hypothesis"* Ronald W. Maris, Alan L. Berman, and Morton M. Silverman, "Suicide Notes and Communications," in *Comprehensive Textbook of Suicidology* (New York: Guilford Press, 2000), 270.

156 *"good correspondents"* Erwin Stengel, *Suicide and Attempted Suicide* (London: MacGibbon & Kee, 1965), 40.

156 *"I feel certain"* Virginia Woolf, March 18(?), 1941, in *The Letters of Virginia Woolf,* eds. Nigel Nicolson and Joanne Trautmann, vol. 6, 1936–1941 (New York: Harcourt Brace Jovanovich, 1980); quoted in Kay Redfield Jamison, *Night Falls Fast: Understanding Suicide* (New York: Alfred A. Knopf, 1999), 84.

156 *"There is nothing new"* Sergei Yesenin, quoted in Kristine Bertini, *Understanding and Preventing Suicide: The Development of Self-Destructive Patterns and Ways to Alter Them* (Westport, CT: Praeger Publishers, 2009), 134.

157 *"I am sorry to cause you"* Suicide letter, quoted in Edwin S. Shneidman, *Clues to Suicide* (New York: McGraw-Hill Book Company, 1957), 203.

157 *"Please take care"* Suicide letter, quoted in Shneidman, 205.

157 *"Take this pen"* Suicide letter, quoted in Shneidman, 205.

157 *"Sometimes this genius"* Paul Celan, quoted in Jamison, *Night Falls Fast,* 77.

157 *The length of suicide notes* Jamison, 77.

157 *They tend to be positive* Jamison, 78.

157 *"There's good in all of us"* Kurt Cobain, suicide letter, quoted in "Courtney Love Reads Kurt Cobain's Handwritten Suicide Note," Far Out, April 5, 2019, https://faroutmagazine.co.uk/ courtney-love-reads-kurt-cobains-handwritten-suicide-note/.

157 **A few have been scrawled** In addition to Jamison's *Night
Falls Fast* and Shneidman's *Clues to Suicide*, I have gleaned
information about suicide notes from George Howe Colt,
November of the Soul: The Enigma of Suicide (New York: Scribner,
2006) and Joiner, *Myths about Suicide.*

158 **"profound insights"** Edwin S. Shneidman, *Autopsy of a
Suicidal Mind* (New York: Oxford University Press, 2004), 7.

158 **"As a group"** Shneidman, 7–8.

161 **"We do not know"** Virginia Woolf, "On Being Ill," *New
Criterion* 4, no. 1 (January 1926): 36, accessed via https://
thenewcriterion1926.wordpress.com/.

168 **The cost of a UNIVAC 1100** "Sperry Rand Is Planning New
Data-Processing Unit," *New York Times*, August 2, 1964, https://
www.nytimes.com/1964/08/02/archives/sperry-rand-is-
planning-new-dataprocessing-unit.html; and John Walker,
"UNIVAC Memories," Fourmilab, accessed January 2022,
https://www.fourmilab.ch/documents/univac/.

168 **A new Buick Riviera** Peter Valdes-Dapena, "8 Very
Valuable Buicks—Yes, Buicks," CNN Money, February 6,
2012, https://money.cnn.com/galleries/2012/autos/1202/
gallery.collectible-buicks/8.html.

171 **"the snow doesn't give"** E. E. Cummings, "i will cultivate
within," in *ViVa* (New York: W. W. Norton, 1997).

174 **more than 47,500 Americans** Centers for Disease Control
and Prevention (CDC), "Facts about Suicide," accessed
September 2021, http://www.cdc.gov/suicide/facts/index.
html. The figures in this paragraph have been brought up to
date to better reflect statistics near the time of publication.

174   *every eleven minutes* CDC, "Facts about Suicide."

174   *130 suicides a day* American Foundation for Suicide
Prevention (AFSP), "Suicide Statistics," accessed September
2021, http://www.afsp.org/suicide-statistics.

174   *Men die by suicide* AFSP, "Suicide Statistics."

174   *an estimated 29 attempts* Suicide Awareness Voices of
Education (SAVE), "Suicide Facts," accessed September 2021,
http://www.save.org/about-suicide/suicide-facts/.

174   *You are two times more* University of Washington,
"Suicide More Prevalent Than Homicide in US,
but Most Americans Don't Know It," Science Daily,
October 30, 2018, https://www.sciencedaily.com/
releases/2018/10/181030102805.htm.

175   *the tenth leading cause of death* AFSP, "Suicide Statistics."

175   *six deeply affected survivors* Harvard Health Publishing,
"Left Behind after Suicide," Harvard Medical School, May
29, 2019, https://www.health.harvard.edu/mind-and-mood/
left-behind-after-suicide.

175   *roughly 285,000 people* SAVE, "Suicide Facts."

175   *highest in the spring* Jong-Min Woo, Olaoluwa Okusaga,
and Teodor T. Postolache, "Seasonality of Suicidal
Behavior," *International Journal of Environmental Research and
Public Health* 9, no. 2 (February 2012).

175   *Christmas season is actually below average* Tori
Rodriguez, "The Christmastime Suicide Myth," *Scientific
American*, November 1, 2016, https://www.scientificamerican.
com/article/the-christmastime-suicide-myth/.

175   *die on a Sunday, Monday, or Tuesday* Gillian A. Beauchamp, Mona L. Ho, and Shan Yin, "Variation in Suicide Occurrence by Day and during Major American Holidays," *Journal of Emergency Medicine* 46, no. 6 (June 2014).

175   *less frequent as the week progresses* Beauchamp, Ho, and Yin, "Variation in Suicide Occurrence."

175   *stone-cold sober* Joiner, *Myths about Suicide*, 91.

175   *a long history of substance abuse* Mark Ilgen and Felicia Kleinberg, "The Link between Substance Abuse, Violence, and Suicide," *Psychiatric Times* 28, no. 1 (January 2011).

175   *whites, American Indians, and Alaska Natives* SAVE, "Suicide Facts."

175   *among vulnerable groups* World Health Organization (WHO), "Suicide," June 17, 2021, https://www.who.int/news-room/fact-sheets/detail/suicide.

175   *Established artists and writers* Kay Redfield Jamison, "Manic-Depressive Illness and Creativity," *Scientific American* 272, no. 2 (February 1995): 66.

175   *the total suicide rate increased* National Institute of Mental Health, "Suicide," accessed September 2021, http://www.nimh.nih.gov/health/statistics/suicide.

175   *"While the link between suicide"* WHO, "Suicide."

175   *Children of parents who kill themselves* Holly C. Wilcox et al., "Psychiatric Morbidity, Violent Crime, and Suicide among Children and Adolescents Exposed to Parental Death," *Journal of the American Academy of Child & Adolescent Psychiatry* 49, no. 5 (May 2010).

176 *"No one ever told me"* C. S. Lewis, *A Grief Observed* (New York: HarperCollins, 2001), 3.

176 *"When I speak of fear"* Lewis, 13.

177 *"one truly serious philosophical problem"* Albert Camus, *The Myth of Sisyphus* (New York: Vintage, 2018), 3.

177 *"psychache"* Edwin S. Shneidman, *Suicide as Psychache: A Clinical Approach to Self-Destructive Behavior* (Lanham, MD: Rowman & Littlefield Publishers, 1993), 51.

177 *"as he lay in the back"* Thomas Curwen, "Waiting for Death, Alone and Unafraid," *Los Angeles Times*, February 28, 2009, https://www.latimes.com/local/la-me-dying28-2009feb28-story.html.

177 *"the stream of visitors"* Curwen, "Waiting for Death."

177 *an accompanying video slideshow* Liz O. Baylen, "Waiting for Death," *Los Angeles Times*, September 16, 2014, https://www.latimes.com/local/la-me-ed_shneidman_ss-htmlstory.html.

178 *Born in Pennsylvania* I have relied upon George Howe Colt's biography of Shneidman's life and career in *November of the Soul* throughout this section.

179 *"We believed"* Shneidman, *Autopsy of a Suicidal Mind*, 7.

180 *"lethality"* Shneidman, *Suicide as Psychache*, 205.

180 *"the probability of"* Shneidman, 205.

180 *"suicidal crisis"* Shneidman, 55; and Colt, *November of the Soul*, 301.

180 *"psychological autopsy"* Shneidman, *Autopsy of a Suicidal Mind.*

180 *established prevention centers* Associated Press,
"Edwin S. Shneidman: Suicide Researcher, 91," *Philadelphia
Inquirer,* May 22, 2009, https://www.inquirer.com/philly/
obituaries/20090522_Edwin_S__Shneidman____Suicide_
researcher__91.html.

181 *"The facts were presented"* Edwin S. Shneidman,
"Some Psychological Reflections on the Death of Malcolm
Melville," in *Lives and Deaths: Selections from the Works of Edwin
S. Shneidman,* ed. Antoon A. Leenaars (Philadelphia: Taylor &
Francis, 1999), 131.

181 *"Malcolm had a deep unconscious feeling"* Shneidman,
127–28.

181 *"pistol shot wound"* Death certificate of Malcolm Melville,
quoted in Shneidman, 127.

181 *"Historically, the mode of his death"* Shneidman, 127.

181 *"The sum and substance"* Shneidman, 128.

184 *"viewing the surface of a continent"* John Adams,
"Programme Note: *Common Tones in Simple Time,"*
Wise Music Classical, accessed November 19, 2021,
https://www.wisemusicclassical.com/work/23702/
Common-Tones-in-Simple-Time--John-Adams/.

186 *I learned that the links* I didn't keep track of all the
studies I read back in 2009, but this 2021 article synthesizes
the current state of research on bereavement and the
body, including the symptoms and effects I mention: Anne
Finkbeiner, "The Biology of Grief," *New York Times,* April 22,

2021, https://www.nytimes.com/2021/04/22/well/what-happens-in-the-body-during-grief.html. Finkbeiner cites this exceptionally helpful paper: Mary Frances O'Connor, "Grief: A Brief History of Research on How Body, Mind, and Brain Adapt," *Psychosomatic Medicine* 81, no. 8 (October 2019).

186   *the first six months* O'Connor, "Grief," 733.

187   *"There are essentially only two kinds"* Edwin S. Shneidman, preface to *Survivors of Suicide*, by Albert Cain (Springfield, IL: Charles C. Thomas Publishers, 1972).

187   *"Those which accrue"* Shneidman, preface, *Survivors of Suicide*.

187   *"suicide-victim"* Shneidman, preface, *Survivors of Suicide*.

187   *"suicide can have on those left behind"* Shneidman, preface, *Survivors of Suicide*.

187   *"The person who commits suicide"* Shneidman, preface, *Survivors of Suicide*.

187   *"The American Psychiatric Association ranks"* Jeffrey Jackson, *SOS: A Handbook for Survivors of Suicide* (Washington, DC: American Association of Suicidology, 2003), 3.

187   *"I would offer"* Edwin S. Shneidman, "Criteria for a Good Death," *Suicide and Life-Threatening Behavior* 37, no. 3 (June 2007): 246–47.

189   *"Ideals are brutal"* Kathryn Bond Stockton, *Gender(s)* (Cambridge, MA: MIT Press, 2021), 62.

189   *Statistically speaking, terminal illness* See J. H. Brown et al., "Is It Normal for Terminally Ill Patients to Desire Death?," *American Journal of Psychiatry* 143, no. 2 (February

1986); and Randeep Ramesh, "One in 10 Suicides Linked to Chronic Illness, Study Finds," *Guardian*, August 22, 2011, https://www.theguardian.com/society/2011/aug/23/suicide-chronic-illness-study.

189 *at least 90 percent of suicide decedents* José Manoel Bertolote and Alexandra Fleischmann, "Suicide and Psychiatric Diagnosis: A Worldwide Perspective," *World Psychiatry* 1, no. 3 (October 2002): 183.

189 *People with bipolar disorder* Peter Dome, Zoltan Rihmer, and Xenia Gonda, "Suicide Risk in Bipolar Disorder: A Brief Review," *Medicina* 55, no. 8 (August 2019).

190 *"around 43 percent"* Jesse Bering, *Suicidal: Why We Kill Ourselves* (Chicago: University of Chicago Press, 2018), 3.

190 *Joiner's theory of suicide* Joiner, *Why People Die by Suicide*.

190 *about 40 percent* Joiner, "Profile: Thomas Joiner."

190 *"The rest of it"* Joiner, "Profile: Thomas Joiner."

190 *"experiences of injury"* Joiner, "Profile: Thomas Joiner."

190 *"trauma can leave a chemical mark"* Benedict Carey, "Can We Really Inherit Trauma?," *New York Times*, December 10, 2018, https://www.nytimes.com/2018/12/10/health/mind-epigenetics-genes.html.

190 *"The idea that we carry"* Carey, "Can We Really Inherit Trauma?"

196 *"A note written to his wife"* "Patterson Funeral to Be Held Tomorrow," *Columbus (KS) Daily Advocate*, March 8, 1940.

202 *"I looked upon the scene"* Edgar Allan Poe, "The Fall of the House of Usher," Poe Museum, accessed March 2014, https:// poemuseum.org/the-fall-of-the-house-of-usher.

203 *"the 'buckle' of the mining belt"* Ben Paynter, "Take a Tour of America's Most Toxic Town," Wired, August 30, 2010, https://www.wired.com/2010/08/ff-madmaxtown/.

203 *more than $20 billion in ore* C. Allan Mathews and Frank D. Wood, "Picher," Oklahoma Historical Society, accessed November 20, 2021, https://www.okhistory.org/publications/ enc/entry.php?entry=PI002.

203 *the companies decided to acquire land* Paynter, "America's Most Toxic Town."

204 *a twentieth-century boomtown* John D. Sutter, "Mining for Picher: Fruits of the Earth Build Up a Town—and Then Break It, and Its Residents, Apart," *Oklahoman*, December 26, 2006, https://www.oklahoman.com/article/2990756/ mining-for-picherspanbrspan-classhl2fruits-of-the-earth-build-up-a-town-and-then-break-it-and-its-residents-apartspan.

204 *"They ought to be"* Orval "Hoppy" Ray, quoted in John D. Sutter, "For Some, Picher Is Just a Faded Love, but at Hoppy's Place, Life Still Has Rhythm," *Oklahoman*, October 15, 2006, https://www.oklahoman.com/article/2956233/ for-some-picher-is-just-a-faded-love-but-at-hoppys-place-life-still-has-rhythm.

204 *In 1983, the town was declared* Mathews and Wood, "Picher."

204　*In 2005, after a high number* Omer Gillham, "Picher Buyout Provides Escape," *Tulsa World*, May 28, 2007, https://tulsaworld.com/archive/picher-buyout-provides-escape/article_a7afaa66-3a95-5652-ac21-00445b66d3fe.html.

204　*"All they want to do"* Ray, quoted in Sutter, "Picher Is Just a Faded Love."

204　*four hundred previously unknown lead smelters* William P. Eckel, Michael B. Rabinowitz, and Gregory D. Foster, "Discovering Unrecognized Lead-Smelting Sites by Historical Methods," *American Journal of Public Health* 91, no. 4 (April 2001): 625–27.

204　*More recent soil tests done* Alison Young and Peter Eisler, "Some Neighborhoods Dangerously Contaminated by Lead Fallout," *USA TODAY*, April 20, 2012.

205　*The Superfund program has struggled* Cheryl Hogue, "Declining Funds Slow US Hazardous Waste Cleanup," Chemical and Engineering News, February 10, 2021, https://cen.acs.org/environment/pollution/Declining-funds-slow-US-hazardous/99/web/2021/02.

205　*Pittsburg was rated* Sarah Frostenson and Sarah Kliff, "The Risk of Lead Poisoning Isn't Just in Flint. So We Mapped the Risk in Every Neighborhood in America," Vox, April 6, 2016, https://www.vox.com/a/lead-exposure-risk-map.

205　*the neighborhood in Minneapolis* Frostenson and Kliff, "Risk of Lead Poisoning."

205　*unsafe wastelands* United States Environmental Protection Agency (EPA), "Pittsburg Zinc," accessed September 2021, https://response.epa.gov/site/site_profile.aspx?site_id=4953.

205   *nearly thirty smelter sites* EPA, "Pittsburg Zinc."

205   *"fail to act"* EPA, "Summary of the Comprehensive
      Environmental Response, Compensation, and Liability
      Act (Superfund)," accessed September 2021, https://
      www.epa.gov/laws-regulations/summary-comprehensive-
      environmental-response-compensation-and-liability-act.

205   *the work is often coordinated* Kimberly Barker, "Former
      Pittsburg Smelter Site Being Cleaned Up for Redevelopment,"
      Joplin (KS) Globe, October 15, 2018, https://www.joplinglobe.
      com/news/local_news/former-pittsburg-smelter-site-being-
      cleaned-up-for-redevelopment/article_d3c5e0f3-c850-5d29-
      be89-463c666ad1c3.html.

205   *Waste is consolidated and capped* Junge and Bean, *Short
      History*, 15.

205   *Pittsburg's Home Depot* Junge and Bean, 16.

206   *At the former Eagle-Picher* Junge and Bean, 6.

206   *"The fifty years of zinc smelting"* Junge and Bean, 15.

206   *When Picher was still alive* Garrett Lewis, "Picher,
      Oklahoma: The Biggest Environmental Disaster You've
      Never Heard Of," 5 KFSM-TV News, November 2, 2015,
      https://www.5newsonline.com/article/news/local/outreach/
      back-to-school/picher-oklahoma-the-biggest-environmental-
      disaster-youve-never-heard-of/527-6b389bed-b0c7-4c67-
      b45a-24402bcce911.

207   *"Sacrifice is a historically"* Wendy Brown, *Undoing the
      Demos: Neoliberalism's Stealth Revolution* (Brooklyn, NY: Zone
      Books, 2015), 214.

208 *more than a thousand migratory birds* Lewis, "Biggest Environmental Disaster."

208 *for many years, sinkholes have been used* Joseph H. Fagan and William D. Orndorff, "Sinkhole Cleanout Projects," in *Cave Conservation and Restoration*, eds. Val Hildreth-Werker and Jim C. Werker (Huntsville, AL: National Speleological Society, 2006), 381.

208 *But in the Mayan civilization* Robert Brinkmann, *Environmental Sustainability in a Time of Change* (Cham, Switzerland: Palgrave Macmillan, 2020), 63; and Samantha Lorenz et al., "The Sinkhole a*s Ch'een*: A Closer Look at Ancient Maya Sacred Geography" (paper, Society for American Archaeology 80th Annual Meeting, San Francisco, CA, April 2015), https://www. academia.edu/34110964/The_Sinkhole_as_Cheen_A_Closer_ Look_at_Ancient_Maya_Sacred_Geography.

208 *"In the language of geologists"* Jon Henley, "What Are Sinkholes and What Causes Them?," *Guardian*, March 4, 2013, https://www.theguardian.com/world/2013/mar/04/ what-causes-sinkholes-florida-man.

209 *"Now it came to pass"* Numbers 16:31–32.

209 *"confirmed that more than a third"* Paynter, "America's Most Toxic Town."

209 *"in danger of catastrophic subsidence"* Paynter, "America's Most Toxic Town."

209 *A 2006 report detailing sinkhole threats* Kenneth V. Luza and W. Ed Keheley, "The Picher Mining Field Subsidence Evaluation and Public Policy," *Oklahoma Geology Notes* 66, no. 4 (Winter 2006): 151.

209   *"It all started with a knock"* Andrew Nash, "Cracks Form
in House as Ground Sinks," *Pittsburg Morning Sun*, March 17,
2011.

210   *"I was having my tea"* Gloria Oertle, quoted in Nash,
"Cracks Form in House."

210   **When Gloria walked out** For my account of what happened
when Gloria Oertle's house began to fall into the sinkhole, I
relied on information from Andrew Nash's article "Cracks
Form in House" and from an interview with Larry Spahn by
telephone call, April 23, 2020.

210   *"We named that operation"* Larry Spahn, in discussion with
the author, April 23, 2020.

210   *"an ongoing problem"* Larry Spahn, quoted in Roger
McKinney, "Galena Cave-in Grows," *Joplin (KS) Globe*, August
2, 2006.

214   *"Call the world if you please"* John Keats to George and
Georgiana Keats, April 28, 1819, in *The Complete Poetical Works
of Keats*, ed. Horace E. Scudder (Boston: Houghton Mifflin
Company, 1899), 369.

Suggestions for
Further Reading

Alvarez, A. *The Savage God: A Study of Suicide.* New York:
W. W. Norton, 1990.

Barthes, Roland. *Mourning Diary.* Translated by Richard
Howard. New York: Hill and Wang, 2010.

Colt, George Howe. *November of the Soul: The Enigma of
Suicide.* New York: Scribner, 2006.

Greenspan, Miriam. *Healing through the Dark Emotions:
The Wisdom of Grief, Fear, and Despair.* Boston: Shambhala
Publications, 2004.

Handke, Peter. *A Sorrow Beyond Dreams: A Life Story.*
Translated by Ralph Manheim. New York: New York
Review Books, 2002.

Hecht, Jennifer Michael. *Stay: A History of Suicide and the
Philosophies against It.* New Haven, CT: Yale University
Press, 2013.

Hillman, James. *Suicide and the Soul*. Putnam, CT: Spring Publications, 2020.

Jamison, Kay Redfield. *Night Falls Fast: Understanding Suicide*. New York: Vintage, 2000.

Joiner, Thomas. *Myths about Suicide*. Cambridge, MA: Harvard University Press, 2011.

———. *Why People Die by Suicide*. Cambridge, MA: Harvard University Press, 2007.

Lewis, C. S. *A Grief Observed*. New York: HarperCollins, 2001.

Prevallet, Kristin. *I, Afterlife: Essay in Mourning Time*. New York: Essay Press, 2007.

Shneidman, Edwin S. *A Commonsense Book of Death: Reflections at Ninety of a Lifelong Thanatologist*. Lanham, MD: Rowman & Littlefield Publishers, 2008.

———. *Definition of Suicide*. New York: Regina Ryan Books, 2014.

———. *The Suicidal Mind*. New York: Oxford University Press, 1998.

Acknowledgments

This book was not easy to write, and the work would not have been possible without the enormous and generous support of many, many people.

Thank you, first, to Patricia Weaver Francisco for helping me find the true book within the one I'd envisioned. Her guidance was invaluable to the conception of this project.

I also owe thanks to these writers who read early and later drafts and offered valuable feedback: Paula Cisewski, Laura Flynn, Melanie Hoffert, Lee Kisling, B. K. Loren, Jane Mead, Jim Moore, Mike Rollin, Sarah Saffian, Pam Schmid, Joni Tevis, and Jan Weissmiller.

It has been an enormous pleasure and privilege to work with Joey McGarvey as my editor; her generosity, intelligence, curiosity, and shrewd editorial eye have helped to shape this book into something I could not imagine alone. She's been a tireless keeper of the book's vision and language: I'm so grateful for her companionship. Heartfelt thanks to her and all the wonderful staff at Milkweed Editions for supporting this project.

Thank you also to Erika Stevens, for early and deft editorial support.

Thank you to my mother and my fellow survivor, Carolyn Patterson, for all things. Gratitude to my cousin Krista Postai, who helped to fill in ancestral gaps and provided me with information, insight, and anecdotes about Pittsburg's history. And to Merton Schatzkin, who helped to answer many other questions.

Thank you to Steve Cox, curator of special collections at the Pittsburg State University library, and to Marilyn Schmitt, a research volunteer at the Kansas Genealogical-Historical Society, who helped me find crucial and elusive documents. And thank you also to the amazing volunteers at the Crawford County Genealogical Society in Pittsburg, who unearthed a lot of historical information about mining in southeastern Kansas and my family history. Thanks also to Marlene Spence, from the Kansas Department of Health and Environment's Surface Mining Unit, for assistance in research.

For thinking about the phenomenon of suicide I am grateful in particular for the work of A. Alvarez, Thomas Joiner, and Edwin Shneidman.

Thanks to John Colburn and Michelle Filkins at Spout Press for their enduring support and for publishing an excerpt of this work as a chapbook, *Epilogue*.

The Minnesota State Arts Board, the Jerome Foundation, and the Loft Literary Center provided important financial support during the writing of this manuscript. Thanks also to the following individuals, who gave generous financial support through a crowd-sourced funding campaign to work on early drafts and research for this book: Stu Abraham, Jeff Bernstein, Scott Bowman, Laurie Brickley, Karla Brom, Barbara Cohen, Sue Crouse, Thor Eisentrager, Rebecca Frost, Frieda Gardner, Melanie Hoffert, Steve Horwitz, Catherine Jones, Michael Kleber-Diggs, Cecele Kraus, Lori

Lahlum, Mernet Larsen, Mary Lewis, Wendy Lewis, Marianne Linnehan, Jim Moore, Kristin Moritz, Donna Partridge, Karen Schultz, Tracy Singleton, Sally Stevens, Kathryn Warneke, Amy White, and Josie Winship.

Deirdre Flesche and her husband, Dag, offered a lovely space to write in a cottage on a piece of restored prairie near Lake City, Minnesota, and for this and many things, I owe them my gratitude.

Appreciation to my fellow survivors: Laurie Brickley, Karen Carmody, Gentry Holloway, and Kristi Mitchell. And to those who supported my physical and psychological health at crucial junctures: Diana Deers, Barbara Fleming, Karen Heegaard, and Eileen Kerr.

Thank you to Kirstin Moritz for her support and generosity.

Thanks, too, to my spiritual sisterhood near and far: Christine Beaumler, Jett Bowman, Olga Broumas, Colette DeHarpporte, Rhonda Dunham, Kelly Dwyer, Jil Evans, Judy George, Felicia Glidden, Beth Hackman, Cindra Halm, Aleta Johansen, Linda Mokdad, Colleen Oake, Margaret Olivier, Judy Ostrowski, Donna Partridge, Katie Pearson, Heid Pliam, Rebecca Richards, Kellye Rose, Sarah Saffian, Susan Scanlon, Lisa Schlesinger, and Mary Titus.

More gratitude for Stu Abraham; Steve Horwitz, a champion of this book from the beginning; Michael Morse, who asked all the right questions all along the way; and Hans Weyandt, who also believed in this book.

I owe these friends a great debt of unending love: Joseph Bednarik, Karla Brom, Kerrie Coborn, Barbara Cohen, Thor Eisentrager, Jane Green, Sharon Jacks, Wendy Lewis, Koebel Price, and Bill Stobb.

Finally, innumerable thanks to Rachel, who makes everything possible. And to Finn, who doubles the possibilities.

Ayanna Muata

J U L I E T   P A T T E R S O N   is the author of two collections of poems, *Threnody* and *The Truant Lover*. Her poems have appeared in numerous literary journals. She has received fellowships from the Jerome Foundation, the Minnesota State Arts Board, and the Minneapolis-based Institute for Community Cultural Development (now the Creative Community Leadership Institute). Her other awards include the Arts & Letters Susan Atefat Prize in nonfiction and the Lynda Hull Memorial Poetry Prize. She lives in Minneapolis.

milkweed
editions

Founded as a nonprofit organization in 1980, Milkweed
Editions is an independent publisher. Our mission is to
identify, nurture and publish transformative literature,
and build an engaged community around it.

Milkweed Editions is based in Bdé Óta Othúŋwe
(Minneapolis) within Mní Sota Makhóčhe, the
traditional homeland of the Dakhóta people. Residing
here since time immemorial, Dakhóta people still
call Mní Sota Makhóčhe home, with four federally
recognized Dakhóta nations and many more Dakhóta
people residing in what is now the state of Minnesota.
Due to continued legacies of colonization, genocide,
and forced removal, generations of Dakhóta people
remain disenfranchised from their traditional homeland.
Presently, Mní Sota Makhóčhe has become a refuge
and home for many Indigenous nations and peoples,
including seven federally recognized Ojibwe nations.
We humbly encourage our readers to reflect upon the
historical legacies held in the lands they occupy.

milkweed.org

Milkweed Editions, an independent nonprofit publisher, gratefully acknowledges sustaining support from our Board of Directors; the Alan B. Slifka Foundation and its president, Riva Ariella Ritvo-Slifka; the Amazon Literary Partnership; the Ballard Spahr Foundation; *Copper Nickel*; the McKnight Foundation; the National Endowment for the Arts; the National Poetry Series; the Target Foundation; and other generous contributions from foundations, corporations, and individuals. Also, this activity is made possible by the voters of Minnesota through a Minnesota State Arts Board Operating Support grant, thanks to a legislative appropriation from the arts and cultural heritage fund. For a full listing of Milkweed Editions supporters, please visit milkweed.org.